THIRTY DAYS IN GOD'S WORD

A Path of Discovery

CONCORDIA PUBLISHING HOUSE · SAINT LOUIS

Copyright © 2021 Concordia Publishing House
3558 S. Jefferson Avenue, St. Louis, MO 63118-3968
1-800-325-3040 • cph.org

Scripture quotations are from the ESV Bible® (The Holy Bible, English Standard Version®), copyright © 2001 by Crossway, a publishing ministry of Good News Publishers. Used by permission. All rights reserved.

Cover image: © GL Archive / Alamy Stock Photo

Manufactured in the United States of America

Library of Congress Cataloging-in-Publication Data

Names: Concordia Publishing House, editor.

Title: Thirty days in God's word : a path of discovery.

Description: Saint Louis, MO : Concordia Publishing House, [2021] | Summary: "The Bible can seem huge and intimidating for someone who has never read it. Where do you start? Even those who use Scripture regularly sometimes find it difficult to understand how it all fits together. This resource will guide readers through the sixty-six books of the Bible in thirty days, providing overviews and historic context of each book and pointing toward God's plan of salvation in Christ. Readers will learn connections between the Old and New Testaments and applications to their lives today as they begin to understand the comprehensive story of Scripture. This Bible resource is designed for youth and adults to gain a basic but foundational understanding of the Bible. Whether readers have spent a lifetime in the Scriptures or have little or no familiarity with the Bible, this resource will make them familiar and confident with God's Word in just thirty days. This book is ideal to give to unchurched friends and family so they can see that Jesus is the heart of the Scriptures from Genesis through Revelation"-- Provided by publisher.

Identifiers: LCCN 2021020628 (print) | LCCN 2021020629 (ebook) | ISBN 9780758669780 (paperback) | ISBN 9780758669797 (ebook)

Subjects: LCSH: Bible--Introductions.

Classification: LCC BS475.3 .T45 2021 (print) | LCC BS475.3 (ebook) | DDC 220.6/1--dc23

LC record available at https://lccn.loc.gov/2021020628

LC ebook record available at https://lccn.loc.gov/2021020629

1   2   3   4   5   6   7   8   9   10   30   29   28   27   26   25   24   23   22   21

TABLE OF CONTENTS

Creation	2000 BC	1500 BC	1000 BC	500 BC
Adam and Eve	Abraham	Moses	David	Daniel

2 BC	AD 33	AD 500	AD 1000	AD 1500	AD 2000	Judgment Day
Christ's Birth	Christ's Death					Christ's Return

The Books of Moses

The Bible opens with five books that were all written by Moses. They teach us about the early years of God's creation, humanity's fall into sin, and the horrible depth of that sin. But they also teach us God's amazing mercy and love in promising to send His Son to save us and establishing the nation from which His Son would come.

GENESIS

❖ CREATION TO 1876 BC

SUMMARY: God creates the universe, mankind fills it with suffering and death, and God announces His plan to restore us.

❖ CREATION   GENESIS 1–2

In six days, God created the heavens and the earth and everything in them. Then, on day six,

> God said, "Let us make man in our image, after our likeness. And let them have dominion over the fish of the sea and over the birds of the heavens and over the livestock and over all the earth and over every creeping thing that creeps on the earth." (GENESIS 1:26)

God's world was perfect; there was no hostility, disease, war, or death. God created Adam and Eve, united them in marriage, and placed them in the Garden of Eden. Their dominion over the earth was kind, beneficial, and caring. Most importantly, our first parents knew, loved, and trusted our loving Creator.

❖ THE FALL   GENESIS 3

God commanded Adam and Eve not to eat from the tree of the knowledge of good and evil or they would die. A fallen angel named Satan came to Adam and Eve in the form of a serpent.

> But the serpent said to the woman, "You will not surely die. For God knows that when you eat of it your eyes will be opened, and you will be like God, knowing good and evil." (GENESIS 3:4–5)

Adam and Eve ate that fruit and lost their perfect relationship with God, with each other, and with creation. Pain, suffering, and death spread through all God's earthly creatures. God had every right to curse them, but in deep love, He pronounced judgment upon Satan and introduced His amazing plan to restore humanity and His creation. He told Satan,

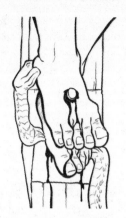

I will put enmity between you and the woman, and between your offspring and her offspring; He shall bruise your head, and you shall bruise His heel." (GENESIS 3:15)

That offspring was Jesus Christ, God's own Son. His suffering and death on the cross (the bruising of His heel) bruised Satan's head, removing the curse and punishment his temptation had brought to all humanity, and condemning Satan, all his evil angels, and all who reject Jesus to everlasting torment in hell.

❖ THE FLOOD
GENESIS 6–8

Adam and Eve's descendants multiplied, but sadly, most rejected God's great promise. Because of their growing wickedness, God decided to purge His creation with a worldwide flood. But He chose a believer named Noah to build a great ship in which God saved Noah's family and all the kinds of animals on earth.

But the flood could not wash the sinful nature from Noah's offspring. As they increased, many turned from God and rejected His promise. So God chose another couple from which He would raise up a new nation and separate it from all others.

❖ THE FATHER OF A NEW NATION
GENESIS 12

God chose a seventy-five-year-old man and his wife who were childless.

Now the LORD said to Abram, "Go from your country and your kindred and your father's house to the land that I will show you. And I will make of you a great nation, and I will bless you and make your name great, so that you will be a blessing. I will bless those who bless you, and him who dishonors you I will curse, and in you all the families of the earth shall be blessed." (GENESIS 12:1–3)

All the families of the earth were blessed because Abram's offspring was the promised Savior. The Lord renamed Abram *Abraham*, which means "father of many nations." Twenty-five years later, Isaac was born.

❖ ISAAC'S SACRIFICE
GENESIS 22

When Isaac was a young man, God gave Abraham a command:

After these things God tested Abraham and said to him, "Abraham!" And he said, "Here I am." He said, "Take your son, your only son Isaac, whom you love, and go to the land of Moriah,

and offer him there as a burnt offering on one of the mountains of which I shall tell you." (GENESIS 22:1–2)

Abraham obeyed God. When Abraham was about to slay Isaac, God provided a substitute ram, tangled in a nearby thicket by its horns. Nearly two thousand years later, God brought His only Son, Jesus, to this same place and sacrificed Him on the cross to save us from death and hell.

❖ JACOB AND HIS TWELVE SONS   GENESIS 29–30, 35, 37

Isaac married Rebekah, who gave birth to twins, Esau and Jacob. God chose Jacob to be the father of the promised nation and changed his name to *Israel*. Jacob fathered twelve sons from whom the twelve tribes of Israel arose.

Jacob favored his eleventh son, Joseph, over the rest.

Now Israel loved Joseph more than any other of his sons, because he was the son of his old age. And he made him a robe of many colors. But when his brothers saw that their father loved him more than all his brothers, they hated him and could not speak peacefully to him. (GENESIS 37:3–4)

Consumed with jealousy and hatred, Joseph's older brothers sold him as a slave to some traders going to Egypt.

❖ JOSEPH RISES TO POWER IN EGYPT   GENESIS 41

The Lord was with Joseph and kept his faith strong, even when he was falsely accused and thrown into prison. Then God gave Pharaoh, king of Egypt, two haunting dreams that no one could interpret.

And Pharaoh said to Joseph, "I have had a dream, and there is no one who can interpret it. I have heard it said of you that when you hear a dream you can interpret it." Joseph answered Pharaoh, "It is not in me; God will give Pharaoh a favorable answer." (GENESIS 41:15–16)

When Pharaoh told Joseph his dreams, Joseph explained that God was warning him of a severe, seven-year famine coming after seven years of abundant harvest. Joseph advised Pharaoh to store up the excess harvest during the seven years of plenty to carry Egypt through the coming famine. Pharaoh placed all of Egypt under Joseph's command.

When the famine struck, everyone went to Joseph for food—including his brothers.

❖ ISRAEL MOVES TO EGYPT

When Israel (Jacob) ran out of food, he sent his sons to Egypt. Joseph tested them, found they were sincerely sorry for selling him into slavery, and revealed himself to them.

> And Joseph said to his brothers, "I am Joseph! Is my father still alive?" But his brothers could not answer him, for they were dismayed at his presence. So Joseph said to his brothers, "Come near to me, please." And they came near. And he said, "I am your brother, Joseph, whom you sold into Egypt. And now do not be distressed or angry with yourselves because you sold me here, for God sent me before you to preserve life." (GENESIS 45:3–5)

In many ways, Joseph was a model of Jesus. Mistreated like Joseph, Jesus was beaten and crucified to take away our sins. On the third day, He rose again and now sits at God's right hand, commanding all of creation. He promises to provide for us until He returns to restore the earth and raise us to new and eternal life.

Genesis closes with Israel moving his whole family to Egypt to live with Joseph. There, Israel's family grew and multiplied for four hundred years.

WHAT DOES GENESIS HAVE TO DO WITH ME?

Genesis explains the origins of our world, sin, and death. It shows God's protecting love as He raised up a nation from which to bring His Son, Jesus Christ, into our world to save us lost sinners.

REFLECTION: *How does God's intimate care for His creation help give direction and meaning to your life?*

DIG DEEPER CHALLENGE:

Read the whole story of Abraham offering Isaac in Genesis 22:1–19. It has striking similarities to Jesus' sacrifice: a father sacrifices his son, the son carries the wood for the sacrifice, God provides a substitute, wearing a crown of thorns.

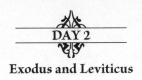

EXODUS
(1876 BC to 1446 BC)

SUMMARY: Israel is enslaved for four hundred years in Egypt. God raises Moses to deliver them.

❖ MOSES' BIRTH
EXODUS 2

In time, the Egyptians enslaved the Israelites. When Israel kept growing, Pharaoh ordered all male babies to be thrown into the Nile River. An Israelite mother placed her baby son in a basket in the Nile. Pharaoh's daughter rescued him.

> When she opened it, she saw the child, and behold, the baby was crying. She took pity on him and said, "This is one of the Hebrews' children." . . . When the child grew older, [Moses' mother] brought him to Pharaoh's daughter, and he became her son. She named him Moses, "Because," she said, "I drew him out of the water."
> (EXODUS 2:6, 10)

❖ THE BURNING BUSH
EXODUS 3

Moses was raised an Egyptian but never forgot his Israelite identity. After killing an Egyptian, he fled to Midian. While grazing his sheep near Mount Sinai, he saw a burning bush. When he came near, God called to him:

> And He said, "I am the God of your father, the God of Abraham, the God of Isaac, and the God of Jacob." And Moses hid his face, for he was afraid to look at God. . . . "And now, behold, the cry of the people of Israel has come to Me, and I have also seen the oppression with which the Egyptians oppress them. Come, I will send you to Pharaoh that you may bring my people, the children of Israel, out of Egypt." (EXODUS 3:6, 9–10)

❖ THE PASSOVER EXODUS 12

Moses commanded Pharaoh to free the Israelites, but Pharaoh refused, even after God struck Egypt with nine plagues. Finally, God sent a devastating tenth plague, the angel of death. He directed the Israelites to kill a lamb and put its blood on their doorframes so that the angel of death would pass over the houses marked in blood and would not kill the firstborn there. At midnight, the Lord struck down all the firstborn males in the land of Egypt. Pharaoh freed the Israelites.

The Passover points forward to the suffering and death of Jesus. In Baptism, we are sprinkled with His blood, so at the final judgment, the angel of death will pass over us, and we will live with Jesus in the restored creation forever.

❖ CROSSING THE RED SEA EXODUS 14

God led Israel out of Egypt to the shore of the Red Sea. Pharaoh changed his mind and sent his army to recapture Israel.

> **Then Moses stretched out his hand over the sea, and the LORD drove the sea back by a strong east wind all night and made the sea dry land, and the waters were divided. And the people of Israel went into the midst of the sea on dry ground, the waters being a wall to them on their right hand and on their left.** (EXODUS 14: 21–22)

Pharaoh's warriors pursued them, but God brought the waters back upon them, drowning the army. God led Israel to Mount Sinai, where He had appeared to Moses in the burning bush.

❖ THE TEN COMMANDMENTS EXODUS 20

At Mount Sinai, the Lord God came down and spoke His Ten Commandments directly to the Israelites. The Commandments were to show Israel their need for a Savior since sinners cannot keep them perfectly. They served as guides for holy living—as they do for us today.

WHAT DOES EXODUS HAVE TO DO WITH ME?

Just as Moses led Israel out of slavery in Egypt, Jesus has led us out of slavery to Satan, sin, death, and hell by His death and resurrection. In Baptism, He made us

God's own people. Now He leads us through the wilderness of this sinful world to the promised land of heaven. He is always with us, and we can always run to Him for forgiveness and help in times of trouble.

REFLECTION: *How can this knowledge bring you peace, calm, and confidence the next time you face a great trial?*

LEVITICUS
(1445 BC on Mount Sinai)

SUMMARY: Leviticus is a worship guidebook for the members of the tribe of Levi, whom God chose to serve as Israel's priests and their assistants. God gave Moses these instructions during his forty days on Mount Sinai.

❖ THE SACRIFICES
LEVITICUS 1–7

God established sacrifices for the various sins and offenses an Israelite might commit. The Israelite laid his hand on an animal's head and confessed his sin. The animal was killed in the sinner's place and its body burned on the altar.

> **He shall lay his hand on the head of the burnt offering, and it shall be accepted for him to make atonement for him. Then he shall kill the bull before the LORD, and Aaron's sons the priests shall bring the blood and throw the blood against the sides of the altar that is at the entrance of the tent of meeting.** (LEVITICUS 1:4–5)

There were six different sacrifices. Each sacrifice pointed to a different aspect of Jesus' sacrifice on the cross in our place.

❖ THE DAY OF ATONEMENT
LEVITICUS 16

The high point of Leviticus is chapter 16, which describes a fall festival. Moses' brother, Aaron, was Israel's first high priest. One of his sons replaced him as high priest after he died. The high priest could only enter the Most Holy Place one day a year, the Day of Atonement. He sprinkled the blood of sacrificial animals—first for his own sins, then for the sins of Israel so they might continue to dwell in God's presence.

Then, he took a live goat called the scapegoat:

> **And Aaron shall lay both his hands on the head of the live goat, and confess over it all the iniquities of the people of Israel, and**

all their transgressions, all their sins. And he shall put them on the head of the goat and send it away into the wilderness by the hand of a man who is in readiness. (LEVITICUS 16:21)

These foreshadowed Jesus' death on Good Friday as humanity's great High Priest. He carried our sins and shed His blood on the cross to atone for all of our sins. When this fall festival was combined with the spring festival of Passover, Israel saw a complete picture of the salvation Jesus would accomplish on Good Friday.

WHAT DOES LEVITICUS HAVE TO DO WITH ME?

Leviticus shows us that worship is a precious gift God gives us. He takes away our sins and lays them on Jesus, who satisfied God's wrath on the cross. Through the Word and the Sacraments of Baptism and Communion, Christ gives us His holiness, strengthens our faith, promises to help us through our daily lives, and reminds us of the eternal home He is preparing for us.

REFLECTION: *How can Jesus' suffering and death in your place give you special comfort when you struggle with guilt?*

DIG DEEPER CHALLENGE:

Read the exciting story of Israel passing through the Red Sea in Exodus 14.

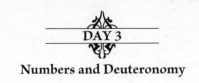
NUMBERS
(1445 BC to 1407 BC)

SUMMARY: Numbers is named for two numberings of Israel. It shows God's faithfulness despite His people's doubts, despair, and open rebellion.

❖ SETTING AND BREAKING CAMP   NUMBERS 2 AND 10

Before leaving Mount Sinai, God commands Moses to count Israel's fighting men and arrange the tribes. God's love of order was indicated by the way He laid out the camp and by the order in which He had them march toward the Promised Land with the pillars of cloud and fire leading them all the way.

❖ ISRAEL'S REBELLION   NUMBERS 13–14

God brought Israel to the southern boundary of the Promised Land and told them to go in and take possession. Moses sent twelve spies, one from each tribe. Ten spies returned with an evil report about the land, spreading fear of the strong Canaanite inhabitants.

> "Why is the LORD bringing us into this land, to fall by the sword? Our wives and our little ones will become a prey. Would it not be better for us to go back to Egypt?" And they said to one another, "Let us choose a leader and go back to Egypt." (NUMBERS 14:3–4)

God was angry at their lack of faith and threatened to destroy them. Moses pleaded, and God answered,

> And your children shall be shepherds in the wilderness forty years and shall suffer for your faithlessness, until the last of your dead bodies lies in the wilderness. According to the number of the days in which you spied out the land, forty days, a year for each day, you shall bear your iniquity forty years, and you shall know My displeasure. (NUMBERS 14:33–34)

Instead, the Lord declared Israel would wander in the wilderness forty years until that first generation had died except the two faithful spies, Caleb and Joshua.

❖ MOSES' SIN

Numbers gives glimpses of Israel's forty-year wandering. One of the worst moments was when Israel grumbled because there was no water. God instructed Moses to speak to a rock, and water would gush out of it. But Moses disobeyed.

> Then Moses and Aaron gathered the assembly together before the rock, and he said to them, "Hear now, you rebels: shall we bring water for you out of this rock?" And Moses lifted up his hand and struck the rock with his staff twice, and water came out abundantly, and the congregation drank, and their livestock.
> (NUMBERS 20:10–11)

God wanted Moses to demonstrate His patience, mercy, and gentleness. Instead, Moses represented God as impatient, angry, and reluctant to do good for His people. Since Moses and Aaron failed to hallow God's name, they were disqualified from leading Israel into the Promised Land.

❖ THE BRONZE SERPENT

A final event in Numbers points to Jesus' salvation. It happened in response to Israel's grumbling and complaining again. This time, the Lord sent fiery serpents that bit and killed many Israelites. The Israelites cried out to Moses.

> And the Lord said to Moses, "Make a fiery serpent and set it on a pole, and everyone who is bitten, when he sees it, shall live."
> (NUMBERS 21:8)

As Jesus later explained to Nicodemus, the bronze serpent represented His death on the cross:

> And as Moses lifted up the serpent in the wilderness, so must the Son of Man be lifted up, that whoever believes in Him may have eternal life. (JOHN 3:14–15)

We have all been infected with Satan's sinful nature, but we need only look to Jesus on the cross in Spirit-given faith that God the Father saves us from the effects of that sin, including eternal death and hell.

What Does Numbers Have to Do with Me?

Troubles frequently drive us to rebel, doubt, complain, and despair, yet God graciously forgives, provides, and protects us. Jesus pleads with His heavenly Father to forgive us for the sake of His own suffering and death and faithfully leads us to our promised land—the new heaven and the new earth, where we will live in God's presence forever.

REFLECTION: *How can remembering Jesus' victory over sin, death, and hell and His presence in your life change doubt to hope and dread to rejoicing?*

DEUTERONOMY
(1407/1406 BC)

SUMMARY: *Deuteronomy* means "second law" and is named for Moses repeating the Ten Commandments to the Israelites in chapter 5. The book consists of three farewell sermons Moses preached to Israel at the end of their forty years of wandering.

❖ **GOD'S FAITHFULNESS IN THE PAST**   DEUTERONOMY 1–4

Moses' first sermon reminded Israel of all God had done for them.

> Or has any god ever attempted to go and take a nation for himself from the midst of another nation, by trials, by signs, by wonders, and by war, by a mighty hand and an outstretched arm, and by great deeds of terror, all of which the LORD your God did for you in Egypt before your eyes? (DEUTERONOMY 4:34)

When we face fears, doubts, and worries, we need only think back to all God accomplished for us in His Son, Jesus Christ.

❖ **TRUST GOD NOW AND ALWAYS**   DEUTERONOMY 5–11

In his second sermon, Moses turned to the present. Israel can trust God to faithfully bring them into the Promised Land.

> Hear, O Israel: The LORD our God, the LORD is one. You shall love the LORD your God with all your heart and with all your soul and with all your might. (DEUTERONOMY 6:4–5)

Jesus quoted this verse when He was asked which commandment was the greatest commandment.

❖ ISRAEL'S FUTURE—AND OURS   DEUTERONOMY 12–30

Moses' third and final sermon looked forward to when the Promised Land would be conquered and Israel would live in peace and security. Moses promised Israel if they would walk in the Lord's ways, they would prosper. Then he warned,

> But if your heart turns away, and you will not hear, but are drawn away to worship other gods and serve them, I declare to you today, that you shall surely perish. You shall not live long in the land that you are going over the Jordan to enter and possess.
> (DEUTERONOMY 30:17–18)

Jesus Christ will return on Judgment Day to restore believers and all of God's creation. When we are tempted to fear, love, or trust in other things besides the true God, Father, Son, and Holy Spirit, Jesus reminds us there is no life apart from Him.

❖ THE LORD COMMISSIONS JOSHUA   DEUTERONOMY 31

Moses' work is finished. God chose Joshua to replace him as leader.

> Then Moses summoned Joshua and said to him in the sight of all Israel, "Be strong and courageous, for you shall go with this people into the land that the LORD has sworn to their fathers to give them, and you shall put them in possession of it." (DEUTERONOMY 31:7)

At the close of Deuteronomy, the Lord led Moses up Mount Nebo and showed him the whole land of Canaan. Then Moses died, and God buried his body.

WHAT DOES DEUTERONOMY HAVE TO DO WITH ME?

When Jesus was tempted by Satan in the wilderness, all His answers came from Deuteronomy. This book warns us against the dangers of sin and reminds us God is always here to protect and guide us. It shows us the blessings of obedience and faith and promises God's grace and forgiveness when we stray.

REFLECTION: *Consider some of the heaviest temptations you face. How can spending more time in God's Word help you resist and find peace?*

DIG DEEPER CHALLENGE:

Read the full story of Israel's rebellion, which resulted in their forty years of wandering in the wilderness in Numbers 13–14.

THE BOOKS OF HISTORY

We now turn from the Books of Moses to twelve books that narrate the history of God's people, Israel, in the Promised Land. They demonstrate the stubborn evil in all our hearts and the amazing grace, patience, and mercy of our God, who sent His Son to save us.

JOSHUA
(1406 BC to 1375 BC)

SUMMARY: At God's command, Joshua led Israel across the Jordan River to begin taking possession of the Holy Land.

❖ CROSSING THE JORDAN RIVER   JOSHUA 3–4

God commanded Joshua to take Israel across the Jordan River when it was flooded.

> As soon as those bearing the ark had come as far as the Jordan, and the feet of the priests bearing the ark were dipped in the brink of the water (now the Jordan overflows all its banks throughout the time of harvest), the waters coming down from above stood and rose up in a heap very far away, at Adam, the city that is beside Zarethan, and those flowing down toward the Sea of Arabah, the Salt Sea, were completely cut off. And the people passed over opposite Jericho. (JOSHUA 3:15–16)

❖ THE CONQUEST OF JERICHO   JOSHUA 6

Jericho was a heavily fortified city with huge walls. God directed Joshua to march the Israelite army around the city for six days in silence. Then, on the seventh day, they marched around the city seven times, and the army shouted.

> So the people shouted, and the trumpets were blown. As soon as the people heard the sound of the trumpet, the people shouted a great shout, and the wall fell down flat, so that the people went up into the city, every man straight before him, and they captured the city. (JOSHUA 6:20)

In the remaining chapters, Israel conquered thirty-one kings in Canaan. When the tribes grew in numbers, they would be able to drive out the remaining people and possess all the land God had given them.

WHAT DOES JOSHUA HAVE TO DO WITH ME?

Joshua reminds us how God keeps His promises. With Jesus' cross, He crushed the serpent's head. We are more than conquerors through Jesus Christ.

REFLECTION: *Through what dangers has God brought you in your life?*

JUDGES

(1375 BC to 1060 BC)

SUMMARY: At the beginning of Judges, the twelve tribes were poised to complete the conquest of the Promised Land—but they failed to drive out all the inhabitants.

> And the people of Israel did what was evil in the sight of the LORD and served the Baals. . . . Whenever the LORD raised up judges for them, the LORD was with the judge, and He saved them from the hand of their enemies all the days of the judge. For the LORD was moved to pity by their groaning because of those who afflicted and oppressed them. But whenever the judge died, they turned back and were more corrupt than their fathers, going after other gods, serving them and bowing down to them. They did not drop any of their practices or their stubborn ways. (JUDGES 2:11, 18–19)

We will look at two of those judges.

❖ **GIDEON**   JUDGES 6–8

Gideon was a very insecure judge who repeatedly sought reassurance from the Lord before going against the Midianites.

> Then Gideon said to God, "If You will save Israel by my hand, as You have said, behold, I am laying a fleece of wool on the threshing floor. If there is dew on the fleece alone, and it is dry on all the ground, then I shall know that You will save Israel by my hand, as You have said." And it was so. When he rose early next morning and squeezed the fleece, he wrung enough dew from the fleece to fill a bowl of water. (JUDGES 6:36–38)

Encouraged by God's signs, Gideon led three hundred men against the Midianites, and God won a great victory for His people.

❖ SAMSON

When the Spirit of God came upon Samson, he had superhuman strength and won great victories with his bare hands. Yet, instead of using this strength to deliver Israel, he used it for his own pleasure and personal revenge. Through his relationship with a Philistine woman, he was captured, blinded, and enchained. But God remembered him.

> **And Samson grasped the two middle pillars on which the house rested, and he leaned his weight against them, his right hand on the one and his left hand on the other. And Samson said, "Let me die with the Philistines." Then he bowed with all his strength, and the house fell upon the lords and upon all the people who were in it. So the dead whom he killed at his death were more than those whom he had killed during his life.** (JUDGES 16:29–30)

In his death, Samson freed Israel by destroying all the Philistine leaders. In Jesus' death, Jesus conquered the devil and all his fallen angels.

WHAT DOES JUDGES HAVE TO DO WITH ME?

Like Israel, we too often forget God when our lives are going well. Then, when troubles arise, we cry out for deliverance. Each time, God delivers us, but often, we slip back into spiritual complacency and sin. Spending time with the Lord in Bible reading, devotions, and worship makes it less likely our hearts will drift away.

REFLECTION: *How much time do you spend with the Lord each day? How can you increase it?*

RUTH
(sometime between 1375 BC and 1060 BC)

SUMMARY: In the dark period of the judges, Ruth shows us God's care for an Israelite family amid a time of their loss and distress.

❖ RUTH'S LOYALTY TO NAOMI

When faced with famine, an Israelite named Elimelech led his wife, Naomi, and two sons to the land of Moab. Their sons married Moabite women, one of whom was Ruth. Elimelech and his two sons died in Moab. When Naomi returned home, she urged her daughters-in-law to go back to their families.

> But Ruth said, "Do not urge me to leave you or to return from following you. For where you go I will go, and where you lodge I will lodge. Your people shall be my people, and your God my God." (RUTH 1:16)

Naomi consented, and the two women returned to Bethlehem.

❖ RUTH AND NAOMI RETURN   RUTH 1–2

During harvesttime, Ruth gathered leftover grain in the fields of a man named Boaz. Boaz invited her to pick in his field among his young girls. Ruth asked him why.

> But Boaz answered her, "All that you have done for your mother-in-law since the death of your husband has been fully told to me, and how you left your father and mother and your native land and came to a people that you did not know before. The LORD repay you for what you have done, and a full reward be given you by the LORD, the God of Israel, under whose wings you have come to take refuge!" (RUTH 2:11–12)

❖ BOAZ REDEEMS RUTH   RUTH 4

Boaz purchased Naomi's property in Bethlehem and redeemed Ruth to be his wife. Ruth joined Boaz in the line of Jesus' ancestors.

What Does Ruth Have to Do with Me?

Boaz and Ruth remind us of Jesus Christ and His love for His bride, the Church. Ruth was a foreigner, and our sin made us foreigners to God. Yet Jesus redeemed us, bought us back with His precious blood and His innocent suffering and death on the cross. Boaz's tender love reminds us of the amazing love of our Lord, our Savior, our Bridegroom, Jesus Christ.

REFLECTION: *How do you think of the people in church? Are they sinful hypocrites or brothers and sisters washed clean in Jesus' blood?*

Dig Deeper Challenge:

Read the account of God encouraging Gideon, the cowardly judge, in Judges 6–7.

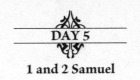

1 SAMUEL
(1060 BC to 1009 BC)

SUMMARY: Israel thought they needed a king like all the other nations. What they really needed was to repent and obey God's covenant.

❖ ISRAEL DEMANDS A KING   1 SAMUEL 8

Israel demanded the last judge, Samuel, to give them a king.

> And the LORD said to Samuel, "Obey the voice of the people in all that they say to you, for they have not rejected you, but they have rejected Me from being king over them." (1 SAMUEL 8:7)

The Israelites would serve human kings, many of whom would lead them astray.

❖ KING SAUL   1 SAMUEL 15–16

God chose Saul to be Israel's first king. Saul started well but over time grew proud and arrogant, openly defying God's commands and directives. Samuel told Saul God had rejected him from being king (1 Samuel 15:23).

God sent Samuel to Bethlehem to anoint a replacement. God chose Jesse's youngest son, David, a mere youth who was a shepherd.

> Then Samuel took the horn of oil and anointed him in the midst of his brothers. And the Spirit of the LORD rushed upon David from that day forward. And Samuel rose up and went to Ramah.
> (1 SAMUEL 16:13)

❖ DAVID AND GOLIATH   1 SAMUEL 17

David became famous for his courageous battle against the Philistine giant, Goliath. When he heard Goliath's boasting, the Spirit filled him with holy anger.

> And David said to the men who stood by him . . . "Who is this uncircumcised Philistine, that he should defy the armies of the living God?" (1 SAMUEL 17:26)

He battled the giant with nothing but a shepherd's sling and five stones. But with God behind him, he would only need one:

And David put his hand in his bag and took out a stone and slung it and struck the Philistine on his forehead. The stone sank into his forehead, and he fell on his face to the ground. (1 SAMUEL 17:49)

Seeing their hero lying on the ground with his head bruised, the Philistines fled in terror.

This brings back God's words to the serpent way back in the Garden of Eden: "He shall bruise your head and you shall bruise His heel." That prophecy was about David's descendant, Jesus Christ. Armed only with the cross on Good Friday, the Lord Jesus went against Satan and bruised Satan's head.

In the remainder of 1 Samuel, we see King Saul's reign degenerating into murderous paranoia as he hunts after David. Finally, Saul dies in a battle against the Philistines.

WHAT DOES 1 SAMUEL HAVE TO DO WITH ME?

Like Israel demanding a king, we sometimes make rash decisions that cause all kinds of troubles in our lives. Yet God is gracious and merciful for Jesus' sake. Jesus, our King, sacrificed Himself to save us from all enemies. He now sits at the Father's right hand in heaven, ruling His entire creation as King.

REFLECTION: *Think of some foolish decisions you have made. How did the Lord deliver you from them?*

2 SAMUEL
(1009 BC to 970 BC)

SUMMARY: In 2 Samuel, David is established as king of all twelve tribes. After capturing Jerusalem, he brings the ark of the covenant into his new capital.

❖ DAVID BRINGS THE ARK INTO JERUSALEM   2 SAMUEL 6

So David and all the house of Israel brought up the ark of the LORD with shouting and with the sound of the horn. (2 SAMUEL 6:15)

This event is similar to Jesus' triumphal entry into Jerusalem on Palm Sunday, five days before He died on the cross. Large crowds welcomed Him into Jerusalem, waving palm branches, singing, rejoicing, and celebrating.

❖ BUILDING A HOUSE FOR GOD   2 SAMUEL 7

David wanted to build a temple—a permanent house for the ark. God had different plans.

When your days are fulfilled and you lie down with your fathers, I will raise up your offspring after you, who shall come from your body, and I will establish His kingdom. He shall build a house for My name, and I will establish the throne of His kingdom forever. (2 SAMUEL 7:12–13)

David was overwhelmed that one of his descendants would be the Christ and that the Christ would be known as David's Son. In fact, that was one of the most common ways people identified Jesus of Nazareth as the promised Savior.

❖ DAVID AND BATHSHEBA   2 SAMUEL 12

David won great victories over many enemy nations, bringing peace all around. But during one of those campaigns, he saw a beautiful, married woman named Bathsheba bathing on her roof. He had an affair with her, and she became pregnant.

David brought Bathsheba's husband, Uriah, back from battle so he would sleep with his wife and think the child was his. When Uriah wouldn't go to her, David gave orders for him to be killed in combat. After Uriah died, David took Bathsheba as his wife. But God was displeased and sent Nathan the prophet to confront him:

"Why have you despised the word of the LORD, to do what is evil in His sight? You have struck down Uriah the Hittite with the sword and have taken his wife to be your wife and have killed him with the sword of the Ammonites." . . . David said to Nathan, "I have sinned against the LORD." And Nathan said to David, "The LORD also has put away your sin; you shall not die." (2 SAMUEL 12:9, 13)

God could have rejected David as king but forgave him with pure grace instead.

❖ DAVID'S CENSUS   2 SAMUEL 24

Second Samuel closes with another tragic event. In sinful pride, David took a census of his kingdom. In answer to that sin, God gave David the choice of three punishments. David placed his kingdom in God's hands, and he chose three days of pestilence. The angel sent by God to spread the pestilence struck down 70,000 men and was approaching Jerusalem.

> Then David spoke to the LORD when he saw the angel who was striking the people, and said, "Behold, I have sinned, and I have done wickedly. But these sheep, what have they done? Please let Your hand be against me and against my father's house." (2 SAMUEL 24:17)

God heard David's prayer and stopped the angel from destroying His people further. David purchased the site where God had shown Himself to David and where David had prayed, and there, David built an altar to the Lord. At that very spot, his son Solomon would build the temple. And opposite the temple, on Mount Calvary, God struck Jesus Christ, the Son of David, stopping the plague on all mankind as He sacrificed Himself on the cross.

WHAT DOES 2 SAMUEL HAVE TO DO WITH ME?

Though David's life was filled with highs and lows, God always protected, forgave, provided for, and blessed him. God is also present in the ups and downs of our lives. Through David's Son, Jesus Christ, God has forgiven all our sins. He calls us to repent and walk in faith.

REFLECTION: *Think of the highs and lows in your life. How has God brought you through both the good and the bad times?*

DIG DEEPER CHALLENGE:

Read the whole account of David fighting Goliath in 1 Samuel 17. Notice the great confidence and zeal the Holy Spirit worked in David to honor God and defend His people.

DAY 6

1 and 2 Kings

1 KINGS

(970 BC to approximately 855 BC)

SUMMARY: The books of 1 and 2 Kings cover the time from Solomon's reign through the destruction and captivity of Israel. First Kings covers the first half of that span.

❖ SOLOMON BUILDS THE TEMPLE   1 KINGS 8

David's son Solomon was best known for the wisdom God gave him and for building the temple in Jerusalem. When the ark of the covenant was carried inside,

> And when the priests came out of the Holy Place, a cloud filled the house of the LORD, so that the priests could not stand to minister because of the cloud, for the glory of the LORD filled the house of the LORD. (1 KINGS 8:10–11)

The same cloud would lower over Jesus on the Mount of Transfiguration in Matthew 17:5.

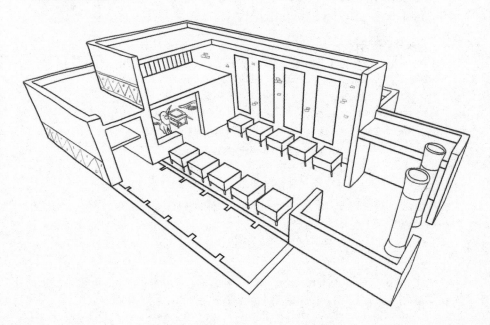

❖ SOLOMON TURNS FROM THE LORD   1 KINGS 11

When Solomon grew older, he turned away from God's laws.

> **For when Solomon was old his wives turned away his heart after other gods, and his heart was not wholly true to the LORD his God, as was the heart of David his father.** (1 KINGS 11:4)

God did not take away Solomon's kingdom, as He had taken away Saul's, because of His promise that David's Son would be the Christ, or Messiah.

❖ THE KINGDOM DIVIDED   1 KINGS 12

When Solomon died, ten tribes rebelled against his son Rehoboam, forming the Northern Kingdom of Israel.

> **And when all Israel heard that Jeroboam had returned, they sent and called him to the assembly and made him king over all Israel. There was none that followed the house of David but the tribe of Judah only.** (1 KINGS 12:20)

❖ ELIJAH BATTLES BAAL'S PROPHETS   1 KINGS 18

Not a single northern king was faithful to God. The worst was Ahab, who slaughtered God's prophets to replace them with Baal prophets. The Lord told His prophet Elijah to hold a contest on Mount Carmel. The prophets of Baal built an altar and spent hours crying for Baal to send down fire, but nothing happened. Then Elijah built an altar, drenched the sacrifice and wood with water, and called on the Lord.

> **Then the fire of the LORD fell and consumed the burnt offering and the wood and the stones and the dust, and licked up the water that was in the trench.** (1 KINGS 18:38)

The people of Israel cried out, "The LORD, He is God! The LORD, He is God!" (v. 39). But the victory was short-lived. Ahab and Jezebel did not repent, and the people of Israel soon returned to worshipping Baal.

WHAT DOES 1 KINGS HAVE TO DO WITH ME?

No matter who governs us, Christ will remain with us, calling us to repent of our sins and trust in His salvation. No matter how far our leaders and nation may stray from God's ways, He will be faithful to us and guide us safely to heaven.

REFLECTION: *Who do you consider the best and worst leaders in your lifetime? How has God led you safely through both situations?*

2 KINGS
(855 BC to 587 BC)

SUMMARY: The Book of 2 Kings goes from the end of Elijah's ministry to the destruction of both Israel and Judah.

❖ ELIJAH TAKEN UP TO HEAVEN   2 KINGS 2

At the end of Elijah's ministry, Elisha watched him ascend—alive—to heaven.

> **And as they still went on and talked, behold, chariots of fire and horses of fire separated the two of them. And Elijah went up by a whirlwind into heaven.** (2 KINGS 2:11)

❖ ELISHA'S HEALING MIRACLES   2 KINGS 4–5

Elisha continued as prophet to Israel. One of his most amazing miracles involved Naaman, a Syrian commander with leprosy.

> **And Elisha sent a messenger to him, saying, "Go and wash in the Jordan seven times, and your flesh shall be restored, and you shall be clean." . . . So he went down and dipped himself seven times in the Jordan, according to the word of the man of God, and his flesh was restored like the flesh of a little child, and he was clean.** (2 KINGS 5:10, 14)

God even raised a child from the dead through Elisha (2 Kings 4).

❖ THE FALL OF ISRAEL   2 KINGS 17

After Elisha's death, God sent many more prophets, but the northern kings and their people refused to repent. God finally sent the Assyrian Empire, which destroyed Israel.

> **In the ninth year of Hoshea, the king of Assyria captured Samaria, and he carried the Israelites away to Assyria and placed them in Halah, and on the Habor, the river of Gozan, and in the cities of the Medes.** (2 KINGS 17:6)

The Assyrians scattered the fugitives, causing the ten tribes to vanish.

❖ THE FALL OF JERUSALEM   2 KINGS 25

Judah was blessed with several faithful kings, but most turned away from God. In punishment, they were conquered by Babylon, the empire that destroyed Assyria.

And in the ninth year of his reign, in the tenth month, on the tenth day of the month, Nebuchadnezzar king of Babylon came with all his army against Jerusalem and laid siege to it. And they built siegeworks all around it. . . . And he burned the house of the LORD and the king's house and all the houses of Jerusalem; every great house he burned down. (2 KINGS 25:1, 9)

Second Kings ends with a glimmer of hope as the imprisoned king of Judah is freed. His descendant will be the promised Savior, Jesus Christ.

WHAT DOES 2 KINGS HAVE TO DO WITH ME?

The Bible has many reminders of Judgment Day, when Christ Jesus will return, such as the great flood of Noah's day and the destruction of Israel and Judah. God's warning for Israel and Judah is the same for us today—repent and seek peace with God through faith in Jesus Christ, our Lord and Savior, before Christ returns.

REFLECTION: *What events make you think of Christ's return on Judgment Day? How does thinking of His return transform your thinking?*

DIG DEEPER CHALLENGE:

Read the whole account of the prophet Elijah's contest against the prophets of Baal on Mount Carmel in 1 Kings 18.

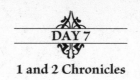

1 CHRONICLES
(Creation to 970 BC)

SUMMARY: The books of 1 and 2 Chronicles bridge the time from Adam's creation to the decree permitting the exiles from Judah to return to Jerusalem to rebuild the temple. The Chronicles were written to comfort and encourage these returned exiles of Judah, who faced resistance and open hostility.

The chronicler's first nine chapters consist of genealogies—lists of names—of people that are mostly unknown to us.

> **And Penuel fathered Gedor, and Ezer fathered Hushah. These were the sons of Hur, the firstborn of Ephrathah, the father of Bethlehem.** (1 CHRONICLES 4:4)

Reading these lists can be tedious. But they remind us that God knows and cherishes the lives of all of His children. They also remind us that the great events of the Bible, such as the flood, the exodus, and the dedication of Solomon's temple, really happened in the lives of real people.

After the genealogies, the chronicler focuses on the reign of King David—especially his contributions to the worship life of Israel.

❖ DAVID CAPTURES JERUSALEM 1 CHRONICLES 11

One of David's first acts as king was to conquer Jerusalem.

> **The inhabitants of Jebus said to David, "You will not come in here." Nevertheless, David took the stronghold of Zion, that is, the city of David. . . . And David lived in the stronghold; therefore it was called the city of David. And he built the city all around from the Millo in complete circuit, and Joab repaired the rest of the city.** (1 CHRONICLES 11:5, 7–8)

The exiles who returned to Jerusalem saw nothing but destruction. But this was exactly how Jerusalem appeared after David first conquered it. Just as David built it into a great city, God would help them do the same.

❖ DAVID'S OPPOSITION   1 CHRONICLES 12

The returned exiles faced opposition and threats from enemies as they struggled to rebuild the temple and Jerusalem. The chronicler reminds them that David spent years hiding from King Saul and facing enemies.

> And some of the men of Benjamin and Judah came to the strong-hold to David. David went out to meet them and said to them, "If you have come to me in friendship to help me, my heart will be joined to you; but if to betray me to my adversaries, although there is no wrong in my hands, then may the God of our fathers see and rebuke you." (1 CHRONICLES 12:16–17)

David lived in constant danger from enemies and traitors, just like the returned Jews themselves.

❖ DAVID ORGANIZES WORSHIP
THROUGH THE PRIESTS   1 CHRONICLES 23–26

With all the work and dangers they faced, the exiles could easily neglect worship and sacrifices at the temple. But the Chronicles reminded them how David made a priority of ordering worship and music in Jerusalem.

WHAT DOES 1 CHRONICLES HAVE TO DO WITH ME?

At times, in our congregations, we can become frustrated by divisions, financial difficulties, dwindling membership, or seeing the influences of our culture invading and turning our people away from Scripture. But 1 Chronicles reminds us God faithfully preserves His people and knows each of us by name. He will see us through all our difficulties and bring us to joy and peace in His eternal kingdom.

REFLECTION: *What difficulties in your congregation do you find most distressing? How can the reminders in 1 Chronicles give you comfort?*

2 CHRONICLES
(970 BC to 538 BC)

SUMMARY: The Book of 2 Chronicles covers the same ground as 1 and 2 Kings, focusing on the Southern Kingdom, Judah, and its kings from the house of David, beginning with Solomon's reign.

❖ SOLOMON WORSHIPS AT GIBEON   2 CHRONICLES 1

Early in his reign, Solomon made a great sacrifice before God.

> **In that night God appeared to Solomon, and said to him, "Ask what I shall give you."** (2 CHRONICLES 1:7)

Solomon asked for discretion to know how to rule Israel. God was so pleased with his selfless request that He gave Solomon great wisdom. The exiles are reminded of God's power working through their prayers.

❖ SOLOMON DEDICATES THE TEMPLE   2 CHRONICLES 7

When Solomon finished building the temple, he gathered all the people, brought the ark of the covenant inside, and offered a dedicatory prayer.

> **As soon as Solomon finished his prayer, fire came down from heaven and consumed the burnt offering and the sacrifices, and the glory of the LORD filled the temple.** (2 CHRONICLES 7:1)

Think of the courage the exiles received from God's presence coming into Solomon's temple. God promised one day the promised Savior would stand in the courts they built (see Haggai 2:9).

❖ ASSYRIA INVADES JUDAH   2 CHRONICLES 32

After conquering the Northern Kingdom, the Assyrians had invaded Jerusalem. King Hezekiah was a godly king who knew he was powerless to stop the Assyrians.

> **Then Hezekiah the king and Isaiah the prophet, the son of Amoz, prayed because of this and cried to heaven. And the LORD sent an angel, who cut off all the mighty warriors and commanders and officers in the camp of the king of Assyria. So he returned with shame of face to his own land. And when he came into the house of his god, some of his own sons struck him down there with the sword.** (2 CHRONICLES 32:20–21)

If God could protect Jerusalem from the most powerful army in the world at that time, the exiles could be confident He would defend them from all their enemies.

❖ KING MANASSEH   2 CHRONICLES 33

Hezekiah's son Manasseh was the most evil king in Judah's history. Yet God even loved a stubborn sinner like him.

> **Therefore the LORD brought upon them the commanders of the army of the king of Assyria, who captured Manasseh with**

hooks and bound him with chains of bronze and brought him to Babylon. And when he was in distress, he entreated the favor of the LORD his God and humbled himself greatly before the God of his fathers. He prayed to Him, and God was moved by his entreaty and heard his plea and brought him again to Jerusalem into his kingdom. Then Manasseh knew that the LORD was God. (2 CHRONICLES 33:11–13)

This had to be a great encouragement to the exiles. Just like Manasseh, God had taken them in chains to Babylon because of their sins. But He heard their entreaty, their confession, and brought them back to Jerusalem to reestablish them.

❖ **THE PROCLAMATION OF CYRUS** 2 CHRONICLES 36

The Book of 2 Chronicles ends with the proclamation of Cyrus, the Persian emperor who defeated the Babylonian Empire.

Thus says Cyrus king of Persia, "The LORD, the God of heaven, has given me all the kingdoms of the earth, and He has charged me to build Him a house at Jerusalem, which is in Judah. Whoever is among you of all His people, may the LORD his God be with him. Let him go up." (2 CHRONICLES 36:23)

WHAT DOES 2 CHRONICLES HAVE TO DO WITH ME?

Like the exiles, you may be burdened by guilt, thinking your obstacles and difficulties are God's punishment for past sins. But on His cross, Jesus Christ already suffered the punishment for all your sins and set you free. He is faithful to His promises to restore, forgive, and make you His own.

REFLECTION: *When have you struggled with the thought that God might be punishing you for some sin? How can remembering Jesus' sufferings on the cross bring you peace in such times?*

DIG DEEPER CHALLENGE:

Read the whole account of the king of Assyria invading Judah and God fighting for His people in 2 Chronicles 32:1–23. Notice the humble faith of King Hezekiah.

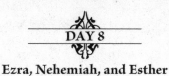

EZRA
(538 BC to 458 BC)

SUMMARY: Ezra describes the struggles the returned exiles faced when rebuilding the temple.

❖ REBUILDING THE ALTAR   EZRA 3

Persian Emperor Cyrus permitted the Jewish exiles to return to Jerusalem. After six months, they gathered together in Jerusalem to rebuild the temple.

> **They set the altar in its place, for fear was on them because of the peoples of the lands, and they offered burnt offerings on it to the LORD, burnt offerings morning and evening.** (EZRA 3:3)

Their enemies were not happy the temple was being rebuilt. As they worked on the temple, there was always a sacrifice burning on the altar.

❖ ADVERSARIES OPPOSE THE REBUILDING   EZRA 4

After Cyrus died, the adversaries charged the returned exiles with rebuilding the city to rebel against the king. The new king, Artaxerxes, wrote,

> **Therefore make a decree that these men be made to cease, and that this city be not rebuilt, until a decree is made by me.** (EZRA 4:21)

Construction screeched to a halt throughout his reign.

❖ REBUILDING BEGINS AGAIN   EZRA 6

After Artaxerxes died, the Jews resumed temple construction. The provincial governor consulted Darius, the new king. Darius found Cyrus's decree and commanded,

> **Let the work on this house of God alone. Let the governor of the Jews and the elders of the Jews rebuild this house of God on its site.** (EZRA 6:7)

The temple was completed without interruption.

❖ EZRA BRINGS A SECOND WAVE OF EXILES   EZRA 7

Five decades after the temple was completed, the Persian king sent Ezra the priest to Jerusalem to restore proper worship and teach the Jews God's covenant.

WHAT DOES EZRA HAVE TO DO WITH ME?

In every generation, God raises up faithful leaders to guide them safely through. Thank God for your pastors, teachers, and lay leaders.

REFLECTION: *Which pastors, church teachers, or Christians has God used to strengthen your faith? Take a moment to give Him thanks and pray for those who serve you today.*

NEHEMIAH
(445 BC to 434 BC)

SUMMARY: Nehemiah was a cupbearer, a highly trusted royal official. He led the reconstruction of Jerusalem's walls after the temple was rebuilt.

❖ THE DIRE SITUATION IN JERUSALEM   NEHEMIAH 1

In the beginning of his book, Nehemiah received a dire message from Jerusalem:

> And they said to me, "The remnant there in the province who had survived the exile is in great trouble and shame. The wall of Jerusalem is broken down, and its gates are destroyed by fire."
> (NEHEMIAH 1:3)

❖ NEHEMIAH INSPECTS THE WALL   NEHEMIAH 2

Nehemiah inspected the state of Jerusalem's walls and announced his plans:

> Then I said to them, "You see the trouble we are in, how Jerusalem lies in ruins with its gates burned. Come, let us build the wall of Jerusalem, that we may no longer suffer derision." (NEHEMIAH 2:17)

Greatly encouraged, the Jews began their work.

❖ OPPOSITION AND PERSECUTION   NEHEMIAH 4

Israel's enemies weren't happy to see the walls being rebuilt. Two foreign officials, Sanballat and Tobiah, taunted Nehemiah:

And he said in the presence of his brothers and of the army of Samaria, "What are these feeble Jews doing? Will they restore it for themselves? Will they sacrifice? Will they finish up in a day? Will they revive the stones out of the heaps of rubbish, and burned ones at that?" (NEHEMIAH 4:2)

Nehemiah prayed to God and then set a guard. Each worker carried his tools in one hand and weapons in the other.

❖ PLOTS AGAINST NEHEMIAH   NEHEMIAH 6

Sanballat and Tobiah asked Nehemiah to meet with them, intending to kill him. They tried to lure him out with a letter.

In it was written, "It is reported among the nations, and Geshem also says it, that you and the Jews intend to rebel; that is why you are building the wall. And according to these reports you wish to become their king." (NEHEMIAH 6:6)

Nehemiah knew the king would never believe these reports. With God's help, the wall was completed in fifty-two days.

WHAT DOES NEHEMIAH HAVE TO DO WITH ME?

God raises up faithful leaders to build up our congregations in the Word and Sacraments and to fill us with love and dedication to Him and to one another.

REFLECTION: *How many of the things that concern you have you brought before the Lord in prayer?*

ESTHER
(478 BC to 474 BC)

SUMMARY: Esther reveals how God preserved His people from certain annihilation.

❖ GOD RAISES ESTHER FROM AN EXILE TO A QUEEN   ESTHER 2

Esther was a Jewish exile who had been an orphan and was raised by her cousin Mordecai. After an extensive process, she married King Ahasuerus, the king of Persia.

❖ HAMAN PLOTS TO ANNIHILATE THE JEWS ESTHER 3

In time, the king promoted a man named Haman to be his prime minister. All subjects were commanded to bow down to Haman.

> And all the king's servants who were at the king's gate bowed down and paid homage to Haman, for the king had so commanded concerning him. But Mordecai did not bow down or pay homage. (ESTHER 3:2)

Haman was furious and plotted to annihilate all Jews, not just Mordecai.

❖ ESTHER AGREES TO HELP THE JEWS ESTHER 4, 7

With his new power as prime minister, Haman convinced King Ahasuerus to make a decree that instructed the Persians to kill and plunder any Jewish people in the empire. Mordecai read Haman's decree and sent a message to Esther.

> For if you keep silent at this time, relief and deliverance will rise for the Jews from another place, but you and your father's house will perish. And who knows whether you have not come to the kingdom for such a time as this? (ESTHER 4:14)

Esther invited King Ahasuerus and Haman to a banquet. There, she revealed that she herself was a Jew.

> Then Queen Esther answered, "If I have found favor in your sight, O king, and if it please the king, let my life be granted me for my wish, and my people for my request." (ESTHER 7:3)

The enraged king executed Haman, giving the Jews permission to defend themselves against those who would enact the decree. The Jews did so and were saved. King Ahasuerus replaced Haman with Mordecai, who governed wisely.

WHAT DOES ESTHER HAVE TO DO WITH ME?

At times, it may seem that Christ is preoccupied with other matters and doesn't seem to care about His bride. But He knows our enemies' plots and protects us from them.

REFLECTION: *How comforting is it to know you don't have to worry about what your enemies are plotting because Christ, your Savior, has it all in hand?*

DIG DEEPER CHALLENGE:

Read the whole account of Haman's fall in Esther 6–7.

THE BOOKS OF WISDOM AND POETRY

We now turn from the Books of History to five books that are among the most beautiful in Scripture. They cover a wide range of human experience and emotion and teach us the wisdom of repentance and faith while pointing to Jesus, our Savior.

JOB

(sometime between 2166 BC and 1859 BC)

SUMMARY: Job confronts the age-old question, "Why does a loving God allow bad things to happen to good people?"

Job was a man of great faith who treated others with care and respect. When God drew Satan's attention to Job's faithfulness, the devil claimed Job only served God because the Lord rewarded him. God permitted Satan to strike Job. In a single day, all his possessions were stolen or destroyed and all ten of his children were killed in a house collapse.

> Then Job arose and tore his robe and shaved his head and fell on the ground and worshiped. And he said, "Naked I came from my mother's womb, and naked shall I return. The LORD gave, and the LORD has taken away; blessed be the name of the LORD."
>
> (JOB 1:20–21)

Satan then claimed Job would curse God if he lost his health. With God's permission, Satan afflicted Job with illness. Job still remained faithful to God.

❖ JOB'S THREE FRIENDS   JOB 8

Three of Job's friends heard of Job's loss and came to comfort him. His friends tried to convince him God punished his children for their sins and is even now punishing him for his. They assured him if he repented, God would restore him.

> If your children have sinned against Him, He has delivered them into the hand of their transgression. If you will seek God and plead with the Almighty for mercy, if you are pure and upright, surely then He will rouse Himself for you and restore your rightful habitation. (JOB 8:4–6)

Their cruel and unjust words failed to convince Job he was wrong.

❖ JOB'S GREAT CONFESSION   JOB 19

Job recognized God's sovereignty and that no one could stop God from doing whatever He chose. Job desired a mediator to argue his case before God. Then he confessed his faith in his coming Redeemer—the Mediator he had been seeking.

> For I know that my Redeemer lives, and at the last He will stand upon the earth. And after my skin has been thus destroyed, yet in my flesh I shall see God, whom I shall see for myself, and my eyes shall behold, and not another. My heart faints within me!
> (JOB 19:25–27)

Finally, God Himself spoke to Job.

❖ GOD SPEAKS TO JOB   JOB 40

God asked Job many questions, focusing on God's workings within creation. If Job could not understand God's workings in creation and nature, how could he possibly understand God's hidden wisdom?

> Dress for action like a man; I will question you, and you make it known to Me. Will you even put Me in the wrong? Will you condemn Me that you may be in the right? (JOB 40:7–8)

❖ JOB CONFESSES AND IS RESTORED   JOB 42

Job realized he had overstepped his rightful place and humbly confessed,

> "Who is this that hides counsel without knowledge?" Therefore I have uttered what I did not understand, things too wonderful for me, which I did not know. . . . I had heard of You by the hearing of the ear, but now my eye sees You; therefore I despise myself, and repent in dust and ashes. (JOB 42:3, 5–6)

WHAT DOES JOB HAVE TO DO WITH ME?

Job reminds us we should not seek God in the wonders of the universe or its workings. Nor should we seek to determine the state of our relationship with God by our circumstances in life. We find God's true heart only in the face of our crucified and risen Lord and Savior.

REFLECTION: *What do you consider the lowest point in your life? How did Christ help you through it?*

PSALMS

(written between the eleventh and the sixth century BC)

SUMMARY: The Book of Psalms is a collection of 150 poems and songs. Almost half were composed by David. The Psalms cover God's works from creation to Christ's suffering and death to His return in judgment.

In the Book of Psalms, God provides us with words to pray to Him in all of life's wide range of experiences—and proper ways to express the emotions that result. In this book, we will classify the psalms into five groups: prophecy, instruction, comfort, prayer, and thanksgiving.

❖ PROPHECY

Prophetic psalms foretell events from the earthly life and ministry of Jesus Christ. Jesus used the opening words of Psalm 22 from the cross:

> **My God, my God, why have You forsaken Me? Why are You so far from saving Me, from the words of My groaning?** (PSALM 22:1)

King David accurately described many occurrences at Jesus' cross, including His hands and feet being pierced, the soldiers casting lots for His clothing, and His great thirst.

❖ INSTRUCTION

These psalms reflect the Ten Commandments.

> **Your word is a lamp to my feet and a light to my path. I have sworn an oath and confirmed it, to keep Your righteous rules.** (PSALM 119:105–106)

David described the true delight of studying God's Word.

❖ COMFORT

These psalms comfort us in our troubles and sorrows.

> **Why are you cast down, O my soul, and why are you in turmoil within me? Hope in God; for I shall again praise Him, my salvation and my God.** (PSALM 43:5)

45

❖ PRAYER

These psalms call on God and include lamenting, mourning, and crying out against foes.

> **Why do You hold back Your hand, Your right hand? Take it from the fold of Your garment and destroy them!** (PSALM 74:11)

❖ THANKSGIVING

These psalms praise and glorify God for all His blessings and help.

> **Give thanks to the Lord, for He is good, for His steadfast love endures forever.** (PSALM 136:1)

WHAT DOES PSALMS HAVE TO DO WITH ME?

The Psalms are wonderful poems that teach us how to pray to God and find confidence in Him in any and every situation we will ever face.

REFLECTION: *Which psalm means the most to you? Why?*

DIG DEEPER CHALLENGE:

Read Psalm 22. Notice the details of Jesus' crucifixion presented here (soldiers tossed dice for His clothing, His hands and feet were pierced by nails), as well as a turn toward Jesus' resurrection, beginning in verse 22.

Proverbs, Ecclesiastes, and Song of Solomon

PROVERBS
(Most were written in the tenth century BC, others
in the late eighth or early seventh century BC)

SUMMARY: Proverbs is a collection of wisdom sayings, mostly from Solomon.

❖ THE KEY TO WISDOM   PROVERBS 1

Solomon explains what he wants his readers to learn from this book:

> The fear of the LORD is the beginning of knowledge; fools despise
> wisdom and instruction. (Proverbs 1:7)

Fearing the Lord means to hold God in awe and reverence. When we approach His Word in fear and reverence, we are wise. All who reject it are fools.

❖ WISDOM PERSONIFIED   PROVERBS 8

In one of his parables, Solomon personifies wisdom as a woman advising us to listen to God's words, which she speaks.

> To you, O men, I call, and my cry is to the children of man. O
> simple ones, learn prudence; O fools, learn sense. Hear, for I will
> speak noble things, and from my lips will come what is right.
> (PROVERBS 8:4–6)

❖ SHORT PARABLES   PROVERBS 10–29

After longer parables, Solomon presents a collection of short, crisp proverbs.

> Riches do not profit in the day of wrath, but righteousness
> delivers from death. The righteousness of the blameless keeps
> his way straight, but the wicked falls by his own wickedness.
> (PROVERBS 11:4–5)

Proverbs closes with wisdom sayings from other writers that were added to Solomon's words.

WHAT DOES PROVERBS HAVE TO DO WITH ME?

Proverbs beautifully explains and applies God's Law to our lives. But God's Law always shows us our sin and our need for the Savior. Proverbs leads us to recognize our guilt and drives us to flee to the cross of Jesus Christ.

REFLECTION: *Which wise teaching from your parents have you found the most helpful? Why?*

ECCLESIASTES
(approximately 931 BC)

SUMMARY: Solomon describes the vanity of his pursuit of pleasure rather than reverence for God. Solomon teaches us how to find meaning and contentment in life.

❖ **ALL IS VANITY**   ECCLESIASTES 1

Solomon begins with the main theme that will ring through his book:

> Vanity of vanities, says the Preacher, vanity of vanities! All is vanity. What does man gain by all the toil at which he toils under the sun? (ECCLESIASTES 1:2–3)

Solomon learned that seeking true joy and fulfillment in life apart from God is vain.

❖ **UNDER THE SUN**   ECCLESIASTES 2

Solomon recalls his pursuit of pleasure apart from God.

> I said in my heart, "Come now, I will test you with pleasure; enjoy yourself." But behold, this also was vanity. I said of laughter, "It is mad," and of pleasure, "What use is it?" I searched with my heart how to cheer my body with wine—my heart still guiding me with wisdom—and how to lay hold on folly, till I might see what was good for the children of man to do under heaven during the few days of their life. (ECCLESIASTES 2:1–3)

In Ecclesiastes, "under the sun" or "under heaven" refers to life detached from God—lived only for oneself. His conclusion? It is vain and meaningless.

❖ THE END OF THE MATTER ECCLESIASTES 12

Solomon ends the book with the conclusion from all his misspent years.

> 𝕿𝖍𝖊 end of the matter; all has been heard. Fear God and keep His commandments, for this is the whole duty of man. For God will bring every deed into judgment, with every secret thing, whether good or evil. (ECCLESIASTES 12:13–14)

WHAT DOES ECCLESIASTES HAVE TO DO WITH ME?

This book is for anyone considering taking a sinful path that seems so much more fun and alluring than God's path of obedience. It also helps us at times when we find ourselves looking back on the sinful temptations that seemed so thrilling and wondering if it really would have hurt to have indulged our sinful desires. Ultimately, it brings us back to Jesus Christ, our Savior.

REFLECTION: *What events in your life have reminded you this earthly life is not forever?*

SONG OF SOLOMON
(Approximately 970 BC)

SUMMARY: Song of Solomon teaches the value of God's gift of marriage and love between a husband and wife. It also gives us a glimpse into the love between Jesus Christ and His Bride, the Church.

❖ LONGING FOR EACH OTHER SONG OF SOLOMON 3

Both the Old and New Testaments use marriage as a picture of God's love for His people and the relationship He seeks with us. Song of Solomon expresses that love and the deep desire between the bride and her husband.

> I will rise now and go about the city, in the streets and in the squares; I will seek him whom my soul loves. I sought him, but found him not. The watchmen found me as they went about in the city. "Have you seen him whom my soul loves?" (SONG OF SOLOMON 3:2–3)

Whenever we pray "Come, Lord Jesus," we should do so with this same intensity of yearning for the day of Jesus' return for us.

❖ DO NOT STIR UP OR AWAKEN LOVE UNTIL IT PLEASES

Solomon reflects God's wise counsel to reserve sexual activity for the wedding night.

I adjure you, O daughters of Jerusalem, that you not stir up or awaken love until it pleases. (SONG OF SOLOMON 8:4)

The joy we will experience when Christ, our Bridegroom, finally returns is an important focus for us. It keeps our thoughts heavenward, where our life is hidden in Christ Jesus.

WHAT DOES SONG OF SOLOMON HAVE TO DO WITH ME?

God unites all believers together as the Church, the Bride of Jesus Christ. Like the beloved bride in Song of Solomon, we long for the day when Jesus will return and bring us to our "happily ever after." Song of Solomon reminds us that we should not give up but all the more earnestly pray for Jesus to come and for God to give us patience until that great and wonderful day.

REFLECTION: *What things remind you of Christ's joyful coming?*

DIG DEEPER CHALLENGE:

Read Solomon's description of Wisdom in Proverbs 8. Notice, beginning in verse 22, how these could be Jesus' own words describing His role in creation.

THE BOOKS OF THE PROPHETS

We now turn from the Books of Wisdom and Poetry to seventeen books that bring us the words God revealed through His prophets. They carry God's call to repent and receive God's grace and forgiveness and foretell the salvation Jesus Christ would accomplish through His birth, life, suffering, death, and resurrection.

ISAIAH

(740 BC to 681 BC)

SUMMARY: The prophet Isaiah was court prophet for the kings who descended from King David and ruled the Southern Kingdom of Judah. The backdrop for his ministry (as for all but the last three prophetic books) is the books of 1 and 2 Kings and 2 Chronicles. Isaiah saw the spiritual rise of Judah under good King Hezekiah and its steep decline under later men from the line of David. Isaiah foretold Jerusalem's destruction and the exile to Babylon, as well as Cyrus' decree permitting the exiles to return and rebuild Jerusalem. God worked through this last prophecy to preserve the faith of the exiles and give them confidence that He would not forsake them.

Most importantly, this book unfolds the life and work of the coming Savior in remarkable detail. For this reason, Isaiah is quoted in the New Testament more than any other Old Testament prophet.

❖ LET US REASON TOGETHER   ISAIAH 1

Isaiah begins by exposing Judah's sin and the wrath of God stirred against it.

> Ah, sinful nation, a people laden with iniquity, offspring of evil-doers, children who deal corruptly! They have forsaken the LORD, they have despised the Holy One of Israel, they are utterly estranged. (ISAIAH 1:4)

Then in mercy, God offers salvation through the coming Savior.

> Come now, let us reason together, says the LORD: though your sins are like scarlet, they shall be as white as snow; though they are red like crimson, they shall become like wool. (ISAIAH 1:18)

This grace of God, to cleanse away sin, sets the stage for Isaiah's prophecies about the coming Savior's earthly life.

❖ A VIRGIN SHALL CONCEIVE   ISAIAH 7

He begins with a prophecy of Jesus' virgin birth:

The Lord Himself will give you a sign. Behold, the virgin shall conceive and bear a son, and shall call His name Immanuel. (ISAIAH 7:14)

❖ FOR TO US A CHILD IS BORN   ISAIAH 9

From there he reveals the divine nature of the Virgin's Son—the almighty, eternal Son of God.

For to us a child is born, to us a son is given; and the government shall be upon His shoulder, and His name shall be called Wonderful Counselor, Mighty God, Everlasting Father, Prince of Peace. (ISAIAH 9:6)

❖ A SHOOT FROM THE STUMP OF JESSE   ISAIAH 11

When Babylon captured Jerusalem, the line of ruling kings from the royal line of David, son of Jesse, was cut off like a tree felled in the forest. Yet after centuries, a new King would arise like a shoot springing out of a dry stump. Isaiah speaks of Jesus' coming and the moment He was anointed as the Christ—the coming of the Spirit at His Baptism.

There shall come forth a shoot from the stump of Jesse, and a branch from his roots shall bear fruit. And the Spirit of the LORD shall rest upon Him, the Spirit of wisdom and understanding, the Spirit of counsel and might, the Spirit of knowledge and the fear of the LORD. (ISAIAH 11:1–2)

❖ BEHOLD MY SERVANT   ISAIAH 42

After His Baptism, Jesus gathered His twelve disciples and began preaching throughout the towns and villages of Galilee, the northern region of Israel. Matthew used our next passage from Isaiah to summarize Jesus' ministry.

Behold My servant, whom I uphold, My chosen, in whom My soul delights; I have put My Spirit upon Him; He will bring forth justice to the nations. He will not cry aloud or lift up His voice, or make it heard in the street; a bruised reed He will not break, and a faintly burning wick He will not quench; He will faithfully bring forth justice. (ISAIAH 42:1–3)

❖ THE SERVANT'S OBEDIENCE   ISAIAH 50

Isaiah also speaks of Jesus' obedience to His Father's will, even the mistreatment He would receive from His own people.

> 𝕿he Lord GOD has opened My ear, and I was not rebellious; I turned not backward. I gave My back to those who strike, and My cheeks to those who pull out the beard; I hid not My face from disgrace and spitting. (ISAIAH 50:5–6)

❖ JESUS' DEATH AND RESURRECTION   ISAIAH 53

In Psalm 22, David gives an amazing description of the events that took place as Jesus was crucified. Isaiah explains why all this had to be:

> Surely He has borne our griefs and carried our sorrows; yet we esteemed Him stricken, smitten by God, and afflicted. But He was pierced for our transgressions; He was crushed for our iniquities; upon Him was the chastisement that brought us peace, and with His wounds we are healed. All we like sheep have gone astray; we have turned—every one—to his own way; and the LORD has laid on Him the iniquity of us all. (ISAIAH 53:4–6)

A few verses later, Isaiah prophesies Jesus' resurrection:

> 𝕴et it was the will of the LORD to crush Him; He has put Him to grief; when His soul makes an offering for guilt, He shall see His offspring; He shall prolong His days; the will of the LORD shall prosper in His hand. Out of the anguish of His soul He shall see and be satisfied; by His knowledge shall the righteous one, My servant, make many to be accounted righteous, and He shall bear their iniquities. (ISAIAH 53:10–11)

Isaiah closes with a wonderful view of the eternal life awaiting us as He describes for us the new heaven and the new earth.

WHAT DOES ISAIAH HAVE TO DO WITH ME?

Isaiah gives us some of the most crushing Law in the entire Bible, exposing our sinful rebellion against our God and Creator and removing any hope of saving ourselves. But then he comforts us with the sweetest Gospel, unpacking very clearly the life and work of our Savior, Jesus Christ, and the forgiveness and salvation He wins for all by His suffering and death on the cross. Whenever we feel broken by our problems in this life or crushed under our guilt, Isaiah lifts our eyes to see Jesus.

REFLECTION: *Which part of Isaiah do you need most right now? Do you need the Law to make you aware of your need to repent and trust in your Savior? Or do you need His Gospel to pick you up out of your guilt and grief?*

DIG DEEPER CHALLENGE:

Read Isaiah's description of Jesus' sacrifice on the cross in Isaiah 52:13–53:12. Notice Jesus' burial in 53:9 and His resurrection, beginning in the middle part of 53:10.

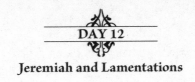

JEREMIAH
(628 BC to 580 BC)

SUMMARY: Jeremiah was a prophet in Judah around a century after Isaiah—before, during, and after Judah fell to Babylon. His was a difficult ministry, for few listened to him—certainly not the kings or prominent people of Judah. His book is filled with powerful words of judgment and condemnation as God tried to turn His rebellious people back to repentance until there was no remedy. But in chapters 30–33, Jeremiah shines the bright light of God's mercy and love and the salvation He offers through the promised Savior.

❖ THE CALL OF JEREMIAH   JEREMIAH 1

Many prophets described God calling them to be prophets to His people. Isaiah saw a vision in the temple in Isaiah 6, for example. But Jeremiah learned he was called before birth:

> Now the word of the LORD came to me, saying, "Before I formed you in the womb I knew you, and before you were born I consecrated you; I appointed you a prophet to the nations." (JEREMIAH 1:4–5)

❖ THE WORDS OF JUDGMENT   JEREMIAH 20

As God's people grew more and more sinful, God sent more and more prophets with powerful words of judgment and warning. Sadly, the people added to their sin by rejecting the prophets and persecuting them. Jeremiah shared his frustrations:

> For I hear many whispering. Terror is on every side! "Denounce him! Let us denounce him!" say all my close friends, watching for my fall. "Perhaps he will be deceived; then we can overcome him and take our revenge on him." But the LORD is with me as a dread warrior; therefore my persecutors will stumble; they will not overcome me. They will be greatly shamed, for they will not succeed. Their eternal dishonor will never be forgotten. (JEREMIAH 20:10–11)

❖ SEVENTY YEARS JEREMIAH 29

When Babylon conquered Jerusalem, Jeremiah's prophecies were proven true. For those living in exile, the ever-present question was "Has God abandoned us and taken back His promises because of our sins? Is it too late to repent?" For the sake of the faithful remnant, the Holy Spirit led Jeremiah to clearly proclaim that God would not abandon His exiled people or make their punishment last forever.

> For thus says the LORD: When seventy years are completed for Babylon, I will visit you, and I will fulfill to you My promise and bring you back to this place. For I know the plans I have for you, declares the LORD, plans for welfare and not for evil, to give you a future and a hope. (JEREMIAH 29:10–11)

This prophecy was crucial for Daniel, one of the Jews in exile who rose to a position of status in Babylon. When the seventy years had passed, he prayed for God to fulfill His promise (Daniel 9), and the angel Gabriel brought God's answer along with a prophecy of Jesus' death.

❖ PROPHECIES OF THE CHRIST JEREMIAH 23

Like Isaiah, Jeremiah also wrote prophecies of the coming Savior.

> Behold, the days are coming, declares the LORD, when I will raise up for David a righteous Branch, and He shall reign as king and deal wisely, and shall execute justice and righteousness in the land. In His days Judah will be saved, and Israel will dwell securely. And this is the name by which He will be called: "The LORD is our righteousness." (JEREMIAH 23:5–6)

WHAT DOES JEREMIAH HAVE TO DO WITH ME?

Jeremiah brings some of the most crushing Law and judgment, but he preaches out of genuine love and concern for the people who stubbornly reject God. He weeps at Judah's stubbornness and refusal to repent. He shows us God's loving heart. He truly does not desire to destroy us and bring difficulty into our lives. He only wants to bring us to repentance and a realization of just how much we need the salvation His Son came to bring. Because ultimately, God wants all of us with Him through all eternity.

REFLECTION: *Think of a time in your life when you stubbornly resisted God. What finally broke you out of it?*

LAMENTATIONS

(Approximately 587 BC)

SUMMARY: Jeremiah also wrote the Book of Lamentations. Remaining with the few survivors permitted to stay in Jerusalem after the exile, Jeremiah looked at the burned-out houses, the ruins of the temple, the shattered walls. He pours out his heart, grieving at the ruin of Jerusalem that resulted from stubborn refusal to repent and return to God. He describes the horrible suffering our sin and guilt bring upon us. But in the middle of Lamentations, in chapter 3, he gives us reason to hope in the coming Savior.

❖ **ALL IS GLOOM**   LAMENTATIONS 1

Jeremiah describes what it is like to remain in Jerusalem to minister to the poorest of the poor, as the vast majority of the people had been killed or dragged into exile.

> How lonely sits the city that was full of people! How like a widow has she become, she who was great among the nations! She who was a princess among the provinces has become a slave.... Judah has gone into exile because of affliction and hard servitude; she dwells now among the nations, but finds no resting place; her pursuers have all overtaken her in the midst of her distress.
> (LAMENTATIONS 1:1, 3)

❖ **THERE IS STILL HOPE**   LAMENTATIONS 3

In the middle of the Book of Jeremiah, the prophet breaks from the gloom to give three chapters of hope in God's mercy through the coming Messiah. In the middle chapter of Lamentations, Jeremiah does the same. Despite all the suffering, Jeremiah points the grieving believers to their God and Savior and His great mercy. Knowing Jesus' suffering and passion for us, we can also have this hope in our desperate times of trial.

> The steadfast love of the LORD never ceases; His mercies never come to an end; they are new every morning; great is Your faithfulness. "The LORD is my portion," says my soul, "therefore I will hope in Him." (LAMENTATIONS 3:22–24)

WHAT DOES LAMENTATIONS HAVE TO DO WITH ME?

Whenever dark and troubling times come upon our lives, we can pray these words to our Lord and call upon Him to deliver us for the sake of Jesus Christ, our Lord. Just as Jesus endured the punishment for our sins and died in our place on the cross, He promises to be with us and lead us through the shadow of death to eternal life in His glorious presence.

REFLECTION: *Recall a time in your life that seemed utterly hopeless. How can Jesus' hours of darkness on the cross give us hope and cheer?*

DIG DEEPER CHALLENGE:

Read the hope Jeremiah recorded for the exiles, promising God would bring them back to Jerusalem to rebuild the city and the temple in Jeremiah 30:1–31:1.

EZEKIEL
(593 BC to 570 BC)

SUMMARY: Babylon captured Jerusalem twice. The first time, they took Ezekiel into exile along with King Jehoiachin (ancestor of Jesus), Daniel and his three friends, and many other Israelites. They exiled all the wealthy, the well-educated, the tradesmen, and the leaders, leaving behind the poorest of the poor. The Babylonians also took many items from the temple but left the temple standing at this time. While Jeremiah stayed in Jerusalem with the survivors, God called Ezekiel to minister to his fellow exiles.

This is when God called Ezekiel to begin preaching.

❖ EZEKIEL'S CALL   EZEKIEL 2

Ezekiel was by a canal in Babylon when he saw a vision of the likeness of the glory of God, which he describes at length in chapter 1. Ezekiel did not see God directly, only God's likeness.

> And He said to me, "Son of man, I send you to the people of Israel, to nations of rebels, who have rebelled against Me. They and their fathers have transgressed against Me to this very day. . . . And whether they hear or refuse to hear (for they are a rebellious house) they will know that a prophet has been among them." (EZEKIEL 2:3, 5)

❖ EZEKIEL PROPHESIES THE FALL OF JERUSALEM   EZEKIEL 4

Since the temple was still standing in those days, the exiles believed they would soon return home. Ezekiel spent his first thirty-three chapters using powerful words of Law to shatter this false hope. He exposes the continuing sins of the kings, princes, priests, and elders who remain in Jerusalem, and announces repeatedly that God will bring back the Babylonians to destroy the temple. To drive the point home, God instructs him to model Babylon's coming siege of Jerusalem.

> And you, son of man, take a brick and lay it before you, and engrave on it a city, even Jerusalem. And put siegeworks against

it, and build a siege wall against it, and cast up a mound against it. Set camps also against it, and plant battering rams against it all around. And you, take an iron griddle, and place it as an iron wall between you and the city; and set your face toward it, and let it be in a state of siege, and press the siege against it. This is a sign for the house of Israel. (EZEKIEL 4:1–3)

❖ GOD'S GLORY DEPARTS FROM THE TEMPLE   EZEKIEL 10–11

The exiles thought God would never permit the temple, the symbol of His glory, to be desecrated and destroyed. When Solomon had first dedicated the temple, the glory of the Lord entered the temple so the priests could not minister. Now, to set the stage for the destruction of the temple, God shows Ezekiel He is abandoning the temple defiled by Jerusalem's sins and idolatry. Ezekiel describes God's glory departing from the temple in three phases. First, it rose up from the ark of the covenant, which sat under two cherubs in the Most Holy Place, going through the Holy Place and to the doors of the temple:

> And the glory of the LORD went up from the cherub to the threshold of the house, and the house was filled with the cloud, and the court was filled with the brightness of the glory of the LORD. (EZEKIEL 10:4)

Then it moved outside the temple, through the temple courts and to the eastern entrance gate:

> Then the glory of the LORD went out from the threshold of the house, and stood over the cherubim. And the cherubim lifted up their wings and mounted up from the earth before my eyes as they went out, with the wheels beside them. And they stood at the entrance of the east gate of the house of the LORD, and the glory of the God of Israel was over them. (EZEKIEL 10:18–19)

Finally, it left the city of Jerusalem altogether.

> And the glory of the LORD went up from the midst of the city and stood on the mountain that is on the east side of the city. (EZEKIEL 11:23)

With Jerusalem and the temple losing God's glory, presence, and protection, their destruction was inevitable.

❖ THE DESTRUCTION OF JERUSALEM   EZEKIEL 33

Ten years after Ezekiel had been exiled, Judah's new king (Jehoiachin's uncle) rebelled again. He broke his promise to serve Babylon and sought an alliance with Egypt. Nebuchadnezzar returned and laid siege to Jerusalem. Three years later, he torched the temple and the lavish homes and pulled down the city's protective walls. The kingly rule of David's line ended as that last king was blinded and exiled.

In Ezekiel 33:21, the prophet records the arrival of the tragic announcement for the exiles:

> In the twelfth year of our exile, in the tenth month, on the fifth day of the month, a fugitive from Jerusalem came to me and said, "The city has been struck down." (EZEKIEL 33:21)

❖ GOD HAS NOT ABANDONED YOU   EZEKIEL 37

From this point, the tone of Ezekiel's prophecy changes from doom to sweet promises of restoration. It was essential because once the exiles learned Jerusalem and the temple were destroyed, they sunk into despair, losing all hope that they would ever return home. They feared God had abandoned them forever and withdrawn His promises—including His promise to send the Messiah.

So God brought Ezekiel to a valley of dry bones. As Ezekiel prophesied, the bones came together, sinews and flesh came upon them, and skin covered them. Then, at God's command, Ezekiel prophesied to the breath and it brought the bodies alive again—a vast army. The Lord spoke to Ezekiel:

> Then He said to me, "Son of man, these bones are the whole house of Israel. Behold, they say, 'Our bones are dried up, and our hope is lost; we are indeed cut off.' Therefore prophesy, and say to them, Thus says the Lord GOD: Behold, I will open your graves and raise you from your graves, O My people. And I will bring you into the land of Israel." (EZEKIEL 37:11–12)

This wonderful promise was fulfilled in the books of Ezra and Nehemiah— God had not withdrawn His promise, and the promised Christ would come as God had said.

❖ A NEW TEMPLE   EZEKIEL 43

Ezekiel ends with a glorious picture of heaven. If the symbol of God's judgment was removing His glory from Solomon's temple, the symbol of His eternal salvation was a new, eternal temple filled with the glory of God—a picture of Christ's return with all the angels in glory on Judgment Day:

As the glory of the LORD entered the temple by the gate facing east, the Spirit lifted me up and brought me into the inner court; and behold, the glory of the LORD filled the temple. While the man was standing beside me, I heard one speaking to me out of the temple, and he said to me, "Son of man, this is the place of My throne and the places of the soles of My feet, where I will dwell in the midst of the people of Israel forever. And the house of Israel shall no more defile My holy name, neither they, nor their kings, by their whoring and by the dead bodies of their kings at their high places." (EZEKIEL 43:4–7)

WHAT DOES EZEKIEL HAVE TO DO WITH ME?

Ever since Adam and Eve were driven from the Garden of Eden, we, their children, have lived as exiles driven from God's presence. But despite our sins, doubts, and trials, God's mercy and love for us remain constant. He sent His Son as our Good Shepherd. Jesus is always with us, guiding us, encouraging us, binding up our wounds, and leading us to our eternal home. When Christ returns in glory with all His angels, He will be the new temple at which we gather to sing God's praises and bask in His glory for all eternity.

REFLECTION: *When in your life have you felt most like an exile? How does the promise of Jesus' return help you through those times?*

DIG DEEPER CHALLENGE:

Probably the most famous passage from Ezekiel is his vision of the valley of dry bones. These are the remains of Israel's hope of returning home—dashed to pieces and left to rot in the sun. Read Ezekiel 37:1–14 to see God's power not only to raise His people from captivity—but also to raise our bodies on the Last Day.

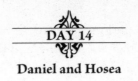

DANIEL
(605 BC to 536 BC)

SUMMARY: Daniel was exiled to Babylon at the same time as Ezekiel.

❖ DANIEL THE WISE MAN   DANIEL 1–2

Wise men were well-educated advisers to kings. We first meet the exile Daniel when he was being trained for that same position with three other Jewish exiles.

When King Nebuchadnezzar was troubled by a dream, he demanded his wise men to reveal what he had dreamed so he could be certain their interpretation of the dream was accurate. Just as God had given Joseph the interpretation of Pharaoh's dream, He gave Daniel Nebuchadnezzar's dream and its interpretation.

> The king answered and said to Daniel, "Truly, your God is God of gods and Lord of kings, and a revealer of mysteries, for you have been able to reveal this mystery." Then the king gave Daniel high honors and many great gifts, and made him ruler over the whole province of Babylon and chief prefect over all the wise men of Babylon. (DANIEL 2:47–48)

You can read about Daniel's three friends and their encounter with a fiery furnace in Daniel 3.

❖ THE LIONS' DEN   DANIEL 6

Decades later, Babylon was conquered by the Persians. God protected Daniel in the transition, and he was given a prominent position in the Persian government, ruling one-third of the empire. He was so successful that Emperor Darius decided to promote him over the entire kingdom as prime minister. In jealousy, the other leaders convinced Darius to decree a law forbidding anyone to pray to any god but himself for thirty days. When Daniel was caught praying to the Lord God, Darius could find no way to spare Daniel, so he reluctantly locked him overnight in a den of lions.

After a sleepless night, the king rushed to the lions' den and called out to Daniel.

Then Daniel said to the king, "O king, live forever! My God sent His angel and shut the lions' mouths, and they have not harmed me, because I was found blameless before Him; and also before you, O king, I have done no harm." (DANIEL 6:21–22)

Daniel was raised to prime minister over Persia, the same position Joseph once held under Pharaoh. With him, God made sure the interests and needs of His people were met.

❖ THE TIMES BETWEEN THE TESTAMENTS   DANIEL 9

The second half of Daniel lays out important visions describing the world events during the four hundred years between the Old and New Testaments. Some included Jesus.

Seventy weeks are decreed about your people and your holy city, to finish the transgression, to put an end to sin, and to atone for iniquity, to bring in everlasting righteousness, to seal both vision and prophet, and to anoint a most holy place. (DANIEL 9:24)

God prophesied Cyrus' decree to restore and build Jerusalem, the troubled time Ezra and Nehemiah describe in their books, and the coming of the Promised Savior to atone for iniquity in His crucifixion.

❖ JUDGMENT DAY   DANIEL 12

Daniel closes with a prophecy of Christ's return and the resurrection of all the dead:

> And many of those who sleep in the dust of the earth shall awake, some to everlasting life, and some to shame and everlasting contempt. (DANIEL 12:2)

What Does Daniel Have to Do with Me?

Daniel reminds us that God is in complete control of His world, no matter how powerful evildoers may become or how chaotic life appears. He keeps His promise to make everything work out for the good of those who love Him (see Romans 8:28).

REFLECTION: *What things in the news do you find most troubling? How does the assurance of Christ's return and His rule in the new heaven and the new earth give you comfort?*

HOSEA
(740 BC to 715 BC)

SUMMARY: Hosea is the first of the twelve so-called "minor prophets." Their ministries were no less important than those of the major prophets—Isaiah, Jeremiah, Ezekiel, and Daniel—their writings were just much shorter.

Hosea preached to the Northern Kingdom during its last days while Isaiah was preaching to the Southern Kingdom of Judah. From an earthly perspective, Israel prospered under its last king, Jeroboam II. But behind the wealth and decadence, the nation was spiraling downward spiritually. It was full of terrible idolatry.

To reach such a secure and self-satisfied people, God gave Hosea instructions that are almost scandalous.

❖ MARRY AN UNFAITHFUL WOMAN   HOSEA 1

God told Hosea to marry an unfaithful woman to reflect Israel's horrible unfaithfulness to her husband, God:

> When the LORD first spoke through Hosea, the LORD said to Hosea, "Go, take to yourself a wife of whoredom and have children of whoredom, for the land commits great whoredom by forsaking the LORD." (HOSEA 1:2)

Just as Hosea had every right to divorce his adulterous wife—and doubtless many Israelite men would have—God had every right to cast Israel away.

❖ TAKE HER BACK   HOSEA 3

God wanted Hosea to demonstrate God's loving compassion and grace for His people, Israel:

> And the LORD said to me, "Go again, love a woman who is loved by another man and is an adulteress, even as the LORD loves the children of Israel, though they turn to other gods and love cakes of raisins." (HOSEA 3:1)

With exceptional love, Hosea tried to win back his unfaithful wife, Gomer. In the same way, God showed great mercy, love, and patience as He tried to win back His wayward bride before it was too late.

❖ WARN HER OF THE COMING DESTRUCTION   HOSEA 5

Hosea warned Israel of God's coming wrath and punishment if they refused to repent and return to Him:

> For I will be like a lion to Ephraim, and like a young lion to the house of Judah. I, even I, will tear and go away; I will carry off, and no one shall rescue. I will return again to My place, until they acknowledge their guilt and seek My face, and in their distress earnestly seek Me. (HOSEA 5:14–15)

Sadly, the Northern Kingdom refused to listen and was utterly destroyed by Assyria.

WHAT DOES HOSEA HAVE TO DO WITH ME?

Hosea reminds us that we are wayward sinners and our Bridegroom, Jesus Christ, patiently calls us to repent and return so He can forgive and restore us. But the time to repent is now—before He returns in judgment.

REFLECTION: *Think of something you have done that causes you great shame. How can Jesus' boundless love and amazing sacrifice assure you of God's complete forgiveness and full restoration?*

DIG DEEPER CHALLENGE:

Read about Daniel and the lions' den in Daniel 6. Notice the similarity between Daniel 6 and Jesus' trials, death, burial, and resurrection.

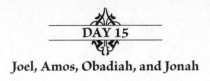

Joel, Amos, Obadiah, and Jonah

JOEL
(date uncertain, definitely after 848 BC)

SUMMARY: God sent Joel to Judah. He compared God's coming judgment to a devastating locust infestation:

> What the cutting locust left, the swarming locust has eaten. What the swarming locus left, the hopping locust has eaten, and what the hopping locus left, the destroying locust has eaten. (JOEL 1:4)

Huge swarms of locusts could strip all the vegetation from fields, leaving starvation and death behind them. Warning of God's coming punishment, Joel pleaded with Judah to repent and return to God before it was too late.

> Blow a trumpet in Zion; sound an alarm on My holy mountain! Let all the inhabitants of the land tremble, for the day of the LORD is coming; it is near. (JOEL 2:1)

Joel also prophesied God's gift of the Holy Spirit, whom Jesus sent to His disciples fifty days after His resurrection on Pentecost (see Acts 2):

> And it shall come to pass afterward, that I will pour out My Spirit on all flesh; your sons and your daughters shall prophesy, your old men shall dream dreams, and your young men shall see visions. (JOEL 2:28)

WHAT DOES JOEL HAVE TO DO WITH ME?

Joel reminds us of the day Christ will return to judge the living and the dead, urging us to run to Christ now to escape God's wrath and punishment.

REFLECTION: *What natural disaster do you dread the most? How can it remind you of God's wrath and His desire for you to repent and be saved?*

AMOS
(792 BC to 740 BC)

Summary: Amos preached in Israel a few decades before Assyria destroyed Israel. The northern tribes were overly confident in their military strength.

❖ JUDGMENT ON ISRAEL   AMOS 5

Amos exposed Israel's sins and warned of the coming judgment. He listed seven of Israel's sins, all involving their mistreatment of the poor and needy.

Despite Israel's horrendous sins, God still loved them and desired for them to return and find forgiveness.

> Seek good, and not evil, that you may live; and so the LORD, the God of hosts, will be with you, as you have said. Hate evil, and love good, and establish justice in the gate; it may be that the LORD, the God of hosts, will be gracious to the remnant of Joseph. (AMOS 5:14–15)

❖ THE BOOTH OF DAVID   AMOS 9

Amos ends with a prophecy of the coming Christ:

> In that day I will raise up the booth of David that is fallen and repair its breaches, and raise up its ruins and rebuild it as in the days of old. (AMOS 9:11)

David's royal line was toppled when the Babylonians deposed them and took them into exile. In the following centuries, no son of David ruled as king over Israel. But God fulfilled this promise, sending the promised Savior whose suffering, death, and resurrection save all who repent and believe in Him.

WHAT DOES AMOS HAVE TO DO WITH ME?

Amos confronts us when we feel prosperous and secure and drift away from God. He reminds us God's judgment is coming and calls us to return to Jesus Christ, our Savior.

REFLECTION: *Recall a time when you drifted away from God. What caused your drift? What brought you back again? How can being in God's Word and worship regularly help prevent these drifts?*

OBADIAH
(587 BC to 553 BC)

SUMMARY: Obadiah was a prophet during the Babylonian exile. His book con-fronted the Edomites (descendants of Jacob's twin brother, Esau) who took great delight when Jerusalem fell and its survivors were dragged into exile.

❖ EDOM GLOATS OVER JUDAH'S FALL   OBADIAH 12

Obadiah exposed Edom's delight in the destruction of Jerusalem:

> **But do not gloat over the day of your brother in the day of his misfortune; do not rejoice over the people of Judah in the day of their ruin; do not boast in the day of distress.** (OBADIAH 12)

God promised to reverse their fortunes. Judah's exiles would return home to prepare for the coming of the world's Savior, while Edom would be conquered and disappear from history.

WHAT DOES OBADIAH HAVE TO DO WITH ME?

Christ Jesus teaches us mercy and compassion for all people because we are sinners who also deserve God's wrath. In genuine love, we share the grace and salvation of God through Jesus Christ, even with our enemies.

REFLECTION: *Describe a time you delighted in someone else's misfortune. How does Jesus' suffering and death on the cross silence that delight?*

JONAH
(Approximately 790 BC)

SUMMARY: God sent Jonah to the people of Nineveh, the capital city of the Assyrian Empire, about a century before it destroyed the Northern Kingdom.

❖ SWALLOWED BY A GREAT FISH   JONAH 1

Jonah despised the Assyrians. Instead of going to Nineveh, he fled in the other direction, sailing west across the Mediterranean Sea to Tarshish. God sent a great storm that taught Jonah and the sailors that no one can defy His will.

[Jonah] said to them, "Pick me up and hurl me into the sea; then the sea will quiet down for you, for I know it is because of me that this great tempest has come upon you." (JONAH 1:12)

God sent a great fish—not to punish Jonah but to save him from drowning. Jesus applied this event to His own life when He said,

For just as Jonah was three days and three nights in the belly of the great fish, so will the Son of Man be three days and three nights in the heart of the earth. (MATTHEW 12:40)

❖ NINEVEH'S REPENTANCE   JONAH 3

The next time God called him, Jonah went to Nineveh and preached:

Jonah began to go into the city, going a day's journey. And he called out, "Yet forty days, and Nineveh shall be overthrown!" (JONAH 3:4)

Nineveh's king and people repented. God had mercy and forgave them.

❖ JONAH'S REACTION   JONAH 4

When God relented, Jonah was furious. God responded,

And should not I pity Nineveh, that great city, in which there are more than 120,000 persons who do not know their right hand from their left, and also much cattle? (JONAH 4:11)

Unique among the lesser prophets, Jonah was an unwilling prophet, wildly successful in his ministry yet resented the success God granted him.

WHAT DOES JONAH HAVE TO DO WITH ME?

Like Jonah, we may be reluctant to share the Gospel with some of the people God brings into our lives. Like Jonah, Christ calls us to repent and see others as He sees them, lost brothers and sisters for whom He suffered and died.

REFLECTION: *What prejudices do you find in your own heart? How does it help to think of how our God looks at all of Adam and Eve's children?*

DIG DEEPER CHALLENGE:

Read the account of Jonah and the fish in Jonah 1–2. Note how God brings the sailors to faith in chapter 1 and Jonah's prayer thanking God for His salvation while in the belly of the fish in chapter 2.

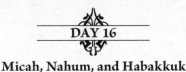

MICAH
(750 BC to 686 BC)

SUMMARY: Micah warned of the destruction coming upon both Israel and Judah and the failure of their kings and false prophets to lead the people to repentance.

❖ JUDGMENT AGAINST ISRAEL AND JUDAH   MICAH 1

Micah begins with three chapters of judgment, especially against the political and religious leaders in both the Northern and Southern Kingdoms. His language foreshadows Jesus' return to judge the world:

> For behold, the LORD is coming out of His place, and will come down and tread upon the high places of the earth. (MICAH 1:3)

❖ THE BIRTHPLACE OF THE COMING SAVIOR   MICAH 5

In chapters 4–5, Micah turns from judgment to God graciously restoring Israel. He makes an important Messianic prophecy predicting the birthplace of the coming Savior. This passage was instrumental in guiding the Wise Men to Jesus.

> But you, O Bethlehem Ephrathah, who are too little to be among the clans of Judah, from you shall come forth for Me one who is to be ruler in Israel, whose coming forth is from of old, from ancient days. (MICAH 5:2)

❖ THE REPROACHES   MICAH 6

Micah's final chapters return to a call to repentance to escape the judgment coming upon Israel. Chapter 6 includes a passage often used in the liturgy of Good Friday:

> O My people, what have I done to you? How have I wearied you? Answer Me! For I brought you up from the land of Egypt and redeemed you from the house of slavery, and I sent before you Moses, Aaron, and Miriam. (MICAH 6:3–4)

Micah closes with a plea to God to show love and compassion to His people.

WHAT DOES MICAH HAVE TO DO WITH ME?

Micah reminds us how easy it is to gradually slip away from the Lord and follow our own sinful path. We need faithful pastors and friends to keep us accountable to God and remind us of our need to repent and trust in Christ Jesus.

REFLECTION: *Think of a joyous, prosperous time in your life. Was it easy to think of God at that time?*

NAHUM
(663 BC to 612 BC)

SUMMARY: Nahum followed up on Jonah's ministry. When Jonah preached to Nineveh, its king and people repented, and God spared them. A century later, another king of Nineveh and his people had returned to their wickedness. Nahum warns them that God will bring the destruction Jonah warned about.

Israel and Judah both suffered greatly under Assyrian brutality and cruelty. Nahum assures the believers in both nations that God will call Assyria to account.

❖ GOD'S VENGEANCE   NAHUM 1

God will protect and avenge His people against their enemies.

> The LORD is a jealous and avenging God; the LORD is avenging and wrathful; the LORD takes vengeance on His adversaries and keeps wrath for His enemies. (NAHUM 1:2)

We are reminded of Jesus' bitter sufferings and death on the cross as the Father punished Him for our sins. Nahum also reminds us of the reality of eternal damnation and suffering in hell for those who reject Jesus as their Savior.

❖ MESSENGER OF PEACE   NAHUM 1

Nahum also proclaims the good news of God's grace, mercy, and love for His people.

> Behold, upon the mountains, the feet of him who brings good news, who publishes peace! Keep your feasts, O Judah; fulfill your vows, for never again shall the worthless pass through you; he is utterly cut off. (NAHUM 1:15)

This points forward to Jesus Christ and all His apostles, pastors, and Christian men, women, and children who share the good news that Jesus has destroyed Satan's kingdom and sets us free to worship and receive the assurance of His forgiveness by Word and Sacrament.

WHAT DOES NAHUM HAVE TO DO WITH ME?

Nahum reminds us that God cares deeply about the affairs of the lives of His children and is actively involved in making all things work together for our good (see Romans 8:28).

REFLECTION: *Think of someone who oppressed you and made your life miserable. How can Nahum bring comfort in such times?*

HABAKKUK
(Approximately 605 BC)

SUMMARY: If you've ever wondered why God allows evil to afflict His people without seeming to do anything about it, Habakkuk is the book for you. Twice the prophet asks God why He tolerates evil—and twice God answers him.

❖ HOW LONG?   HABAKKUK 1

Habakkuk sees injustice and violence persisting around him in Judah, and God seems to do nothing about it. So Habakkuk raises his complaint to the Lord and asks,

> O LORD, how long shall I cry for help, and You will not hear? Or cry to You, "Violence!" and You will not save? (HABAKKUK 1:2)

God answers,

> For behold, I am raising up the Chaldeans, that bitter and hasty nation, who march through the breadth of the earth, to seize dwellings not their own. (HABAKKUK 1:6)

The Chaldeans were one of the main elements of the Babylonian Empire. God would call in the Babylonians to end the injustice in Judah.

❖ HABAKKUK'S SECOND QUESTION   HABAKKUK 1

The prophet is stunned. He wants righteousness to prevail—but not via invasion by a more unjust and cruel nation. He asks,

THIRTY DAYS IN GOD'S WORD

You who are of purer eyes than to see evil and cannot look at wrong, why do You idly look at traitors and remain silent when the wicked swallows up the man more righteous than he? (HABAKKUK 1:13)

❖ THE RIGHTEOUS SHALL LIVE BY FAITH   HABAKKUK 2

When we see evildoers prosper, God teaches us to trust Him and His promise to restore His people. Speaking of the Babylonians, God tells Habakkuk,

Behold, his soul is puffed up; it is not upright within him, but the righteous shall live by his faith. (HABAKKUK 2:4)

Faith is believing God will keep His promises. He will punish sin and evildoers and rescue believers who trust in Him through Jesus Christ. Clinging to God's promise, strengthened by Word and Sacrament, we wait for God's deliverance.

WHAT DOES HABAKKUK HAVE TO DO WITH ME?

All of us are afflicted by sin and sinners in this world. When we see evildoers prosper, we may question God's justice or the use in serving Him. Habakkuk reminds us that God is slow to anger because He is giving the sinner time to repent, but in His time, He will reward the godly and punish the evildoer.

REFLECTION: *Think of a situation that made you question God's righteousness. How could the message of Habakkuk give you patience and hope?*

DIG DEEPER CHALLENGE:

Read Micah's prophecy of Christ's birth in Bethlehem in Micah 5:1–5. Notice how Christ's origins "from ancient days" refer to Him being begotten in eternity before creation, the only Son of the Father.

ZEPHANIAH
(640–609 BC)

SUMMARY: Zephaniah warned Judah to repent or be conquered by Babylon.

❖ THE DAY OF THE LORD   ZEPHANIAH 1

Zephaniah warns of "the day of the LORD," the day Jerusalem fell to Babylon. But ultimately, the prophet speaks of Judgment Day when Christ will return:

> I will utterly sweep away everything from the face of the earth," declares the LORD. . . . Be silent before the Lord GOD! For the day of the LORD is near; the LORD has prepared a sacrifice and consecrated His guests. (ZEPHANIAH 1:2, 7)

❖ WISDOM PERSONIFIED   ZEPHANIAH 3

The judgment Zephaniah portrays is terrifying, but he comforts believers with the Gospel, promising salvation to those who trust in the coming Messiah.

> Sing aloud, O daughter of Zion; shout, O Israel! Rejoice and exult with all your heart, O daughter of Jerusalem! The LORD has taken away the judgments against you; He has cleared away your enemies. The King of Israel, the LORD, is in your midst; you shall never again fear evil. (ZEPHANIAH 3:14–15)

WHAT DOES ZEPHANIAH HAVE TO DO WITH ME?

Zephaniah reminds us that Jesus will return on Judgment Day to perfect His entire creation. He will remove all unbelievers from His creation and give believers eternal life in His presence. Now is the time to repent and flee to Him.

REFLECTION: *Think of things in this world that are not right. How does thinking of Jesus returning and cleansing creation give you hope and joy?*

HAGGAI
(520 BC)

SUMMARY: Haggai spoke to the returned exiles who were building the temple. After King Artaxerxes died (who had commanded all work on the temple to stop), Haggai encouraged the exiles to resume constructing the temple in Jerusalem.

❖ MISPLACED PRIORITIES
HAGGAI 1

The returned exiles were sure the temple would never be completed. So they focused instead on their homes, farms, orchards, and vineyards. Haggai told them,

> You looked for much, and behold, it came to little. And when you brought it home, I blew it away. Why? declares the LORD of hosts. Because of My house that lies in ruins, while each of you busies himself with his own house. (HAGGAI 1:9)

After three months, he was joined by Zechariah. Encouraged by these two prophets, the exiles completed the temple.

❖ THE GLORY OF THIS HOUSE WILL SURPASS THE LAST
HAGGAI 2

To the oldest exiles who had seen the splendor of Solomon's golden temple, this new temple was a bitter disappointment. Haggai addressed their misconception.

> The latter glory of this house shall be greater than the former, says the LORD of hosts. And in this place I will give peace, declares the LORD of hosts. (HAGGAI 2:9)

The prophet speaks of Jesus' appearance in this temple—as a twelve-year-old and during His public ministry. And opposite the temple, just outside the city walls, God would give peace through Jesus' suffering and death on the cross.

WHAT DOES HAGGAI HAVE TO DO WITH ME?

Our congregations may seem like insignificant people meeting in lowly houses of worship, but there we meet Christ, hear His Word, and receive His peace and forgiveness through His Word and Sacraments.

REFLECTION: *When you think of your church family, what do you see—a dysfunctional family or brothers and sisters washed in the blood of Jesus Christ?*

ZECHARIAH
(520 BC to 518 BC)

SUMMARY: Haggai and Zechariah encouraged the returned exiles to finish rebuilding the temple. Then Zechariah gave specific details about Jesus' life.

❖ **PREDICTIONS OF JESUS' LIFE**   ZECHARIAH 9–12

Zechariah gives three startling predictions of events from the week leading up to Jesus' death. He begins with Jesus' triumphal entry into Jerusalem on Palm Sunday:

> Rejoice greatly, O daughter of Zion! Shout aloud, O daughter of Jerusalem! Behold, your King is coming to you; righteous and having salvation is He, humble and mounted on a donkey, on a colt, the foal of a donkey. (ZECHARIAH 9:9)

Next, he speaks of Judas's betrayal. He even mentions Judas throwing that money into the temple and the priests buying a burial field from the potter:

> Then I said to them, "If it seems good to you, give me my wages; but if not, keep them." And they weighed out as my wages thirty pieces of silver. Then the LORD said to me, "Throw it to the potter"—the lordly price at which I was priced by them. So I took the thirty pieces of silver and threw them into the house of the LORD, to the potter. (ZECHARIAH 11:12–13)

Finally, he speaks of Jesus being pierced—His hands and feet by nails and His side with a spear:

> And I will pour out on the house of David and the inhabitants of Jerusalem a spirit of grace and pleas for mercy, so that, when they look on Me, on Him whom they have pierced, they shall mourn for Him, as one mourns for an only child, and weep bitterly over Him, as one weeps over a firstborn. (ZECHARIAH 12:10)

WHAT DOES ZECHARIAH HAVE TO DO WITH ME?

This book shows God's great wrath against our sin but reminds us of His greater mercy, love, and forgiveness won by the suffering and death of our Lord, Jesus Christ.

REFLECTION: *What do you feel is your greatest need today? How does God's promise to answer that need give you hope?*

MALACHI
(Approximately 430 BC)

SUMMARY: The temple has been rebuilt, but apathy fills the people and the priests. Malachi begins with the priests' lax attitude toward sacrifices, calling the priests and people to repent.

❖ THE MESSENGER OF THE COVENANT   MALACHI 3

Malachi predicts the coming Savior, the "messenger of the covenant":

> Behold, I send My messenger, and he will prepare the way before Me. And the Lord whom you seek will suddenly come to His temple; and the messenger of the covenant in whom you delight, behold, He is coming, says the LORD of hosts. (MALACHI 3:1)

❖ ELIJAH THE PROPHET   MALACHI 4

Malachi ends with a bold and wonderful promise:

> Behold, I will send you Elijah the prophet before the great and awesome day of the LORD comes. (MALACHI 4:5)

This prophecy about John the Baptist reveals the promised Savior is near.

WHAT DOES MALACHI HAVE TO DO WITH ME?

Examine your relationship with God. Do you truly offer your life to Him or only your spare time, talent, and money? Christ has come to call us to repentance, forgive our sins, and draw us to a closer relationship with God, our heavenly Father.

REFLECTION: *If you knew Christ would return tomorrow, how would it change your attitude toward your life today?*

DIG DEEPER CHALLENGE:

Read Malachi's prophecy of the coming ministries of John the Baptist and Jesus in Malachi 3:1–4.

The Gospels

We have worked through all the books of the Old Testament. The New Testament opens with four books that bring the Good News—the Gospel—of God's Son, Jesus Christ, and His mission to save us from our sins. This is the very heart of Scripture.

MATTHEW
(2 BC to AD 33)

SUMMARY: Each Gospel writer shared the life and work of Jesus Christ for a different audience with a slightly different emphasis. Matthew was a tax collector Jesus called to be one of His twelve apostles. Matthew wrote to show the Jews how Jesus fulfilled the Old Testament prophecies, proving He was the promised Savior.

❖ JESUS' GENEALOGY   MATTHEW 1

To prove Jesus was the Messiah, it was essential for Matthew to show Jesus was a descendant of Abraham, Isaac, Jacob, and King David because God had promised each of these believers that the Christ would come from their lines. So he begins his Gospel:

> The book of the genealogy of Jesus Christ, the son of David, the son of Abraham. (MATTHEW 1:1)

❖ BORN OF A VIRGIN IN BETHLEHEM   MATTHEW 2

Matthew next turns to Jesus' birth and childhood, which fulfill two Old Testament prophecies. The first related to Jesus' mother, Mary, and how she could be the mother of the Son of God while she was still a virgin:

> All this took place to fulfill what the Lord had spoken by the prophet: "Behold, the virgin shall conceive and bear a son, and they shall call His name Immanuel (which means, God with us)."
> (MATTHEW 1:22–23)

Jesus was known as "Jesus of Nazareth." The Jews protested that the Christ was to be born in Bethlehem, not Nazareth. Matthew's account of the visit of the Wise Men explains. When they arrived in Jerusalem, King Herod consulted the chief priests and scribes, who answered from the Book of Micah:

> They told him, "In Bethlehem of Judea, for so it is written by the prophet." (MATTHEW 2:5)

Matthew then explained how the Wise Men offered their gifts to Jesus but after being warned in a dream, they didn't return to Herod. In rage, the paranoid king ordered all boys two years old and under to be killed. After being warned in a dream, Joseph took Mary and Jesus to Egypt and raised Jesus in Nazareth rather than Bethlehem. Otherwise, it is possible Jesus would have been known as "Jesus of Bethlehem."

❖ JESUS' MINISTRY   MATTHEW 4–20

When Jesus reached the age of thirty, He was baptized by John the Baptist. God the Father spoke, and the Holy Spirit descended upon Jesus in the form of a dove, making Him the Christ or the "Anointed One." This marked the beginning of Jesus' public ministry. After recording Jesus' Sermon on the Mount in chapters 5–7, Matthew describes a variety of healing miracles Jesus worked. Again, Matthew points out that this is precisely what the Old Testament foretold:

> This was to fulfill what was spoken by the prophet Isaiah: "He took our illnesses and bore our diseases."
> (MATTHEW 8:17)

Next, Matthew turns to Jesus' teachings. When Jesus' disciples asked Him why He was teaching in parables, He quoted Isaiah:

> This is why I speak to them in parables, because seeing they do not see, and hearing they do not hear, nor do they understand. Indeed, in their case the prophecy of Isaiah is fulfilled that says: "You will indeed hear but never understand, and you will indeed see but never perceive." (MATTHEW 13:13–14)

Matthew 16:16 marks a turning point in Jesus' ministry. Peter confesses that Jesus is the Christ, the Son of God. At that point, Jesus begins predicting and teaching them about His coming death and resurrection. Matthew records three of these predictions. Here is the first:

> From that time Jesus began to show His disciples that He must go to Jerusalem and suffer many things from the elders and chief

priests and scribes, and be killed, and on the third day be raised. (MATTHEW 16:21)

Not long after giving His first prediction, Jesus was transfigured before three of the disciples. He revealed His glory as God's Son through His human body.

❖ HOLY WEEK   MATTHEW 21–26

On the Sunday before His death, Jesus rode into Jerusalem in triumph. Matthew points out this fulfilled yet another Old Testament prophecy, this time from Zechariah:

> This took place to fulfill what was spoken by the prophet, saying, "Say to the daughter of Zion, Behold, your king is coming to you, humble, and mounted on a donkey, on a colt, the foal of a beast of burden." (MATTHEW 21:4–5)

Throughout the last week before Jesus' death, He faced intense scrutiny and questioning from the Jewish religious leaders. Finally, He silenced them with a question based on David's words in Psalm 110:

> Saying, "What do you think about the Christ? Whose son is He?" They said to Him, "The son of David." He said to them, "How is it then that David, in the Spirit, calls Him Lord, saying, 'The Lord said to my Lord, Sit at My right hand, until I put Your enemies under Your feet.' If then David calls Him Lord, how is He his son?" (MATTHEW 22:42–45)

❖ JESUS' CRUCIFIXION   MATTHEW 27

Matthew gives a full account of Jesus' trials before the Jewish religious leaders and Pontius Pilate, the Roman leader we will discuss in more detail in the following Gospels. One important event only Matthew gives is what happened to Jesus' betrayer, Judas Iscariot, one of Jesus' chosen twelve—and how its details were foretold in amazing detail in the Book of Zechariah in the Old Testament.

Judas betrayed Jesus for thirty silver pieces then felt deep remorse when he learned Jesus was condemned. He brought the silver back to the Jewish leaders. When they snubbed him, he threw the silver in the temple and went out and hanged himself. The chief priests considered the silver "blood money" and used it to purchase a field from a potter to bury strangers. Matthew points out how this fulfilled prophecies from Jeremiah and Zechariah.

> Then was fulfilled what had been spoken by the prophet Jeremiah, saying, "And they took the thirty pieces of silver, the price of Him

on whom a price had been set by some of the sons of Israel, and they gave them for the potter's field, as the Lord directed me. (MATTHEW 27:9–10)

The four Gospels record seven sayings Jesus spoke from the cross. Matthew only recorded one, from the first verse of David's familiar Psalm 22:

And about the ninth hour Jesus cried out with a loud voice, saying, "Eli, Eli, lema sabachthani?" that is, "My God, My God, why have You forsaken Me?" (MATTHEW 27:46)

This verse would have made Jews think of the entire psalm, which gives striking details of the crucifixion. These include how the soldiers divided Jesus' clothing among them, cast lots for His outer garment, and pierced His hands and His feet with the nails.

❖ JESUS' RESURRECTION   MATTHEW 28

Matthew's account of Jesus' resurrection is interesting. One of Matthew's biggest challenges was the widely believed story circulating among the Jews of his day that Jesus' disciples had stolen His body and then claimed He had risen from the dead. Matthew explains that the guards were set in place precisely to prevent Jesus' disciples from stealing the body. When the angel came and rolled the stone away, the guards saw the tomb was empty and ran back to report to the Jewish chief priests, who bribed them to say they had fallen asleep and the disciples stole the body. Matthew's account reveals how far-fetched this story really is.

WHAT DOES MATTHEW HAVE TO DO WITH ME?

We don't have to be Jewish to appreciate the Gospel of Matthew. It shows that Jesus Christ, the Savior of the nations, has completely fulfilled the prophecies God gave throughout the Old Testament. We can be confident to call upon Him for peace, grace, and forgiveness.

REFLECTION: Who do you think Jesus is?

DIG DEEPER CHALLENGE:

Read Matthew's account of Jesus' resurrection in Matthew 28:1–10. Notice the angel reminding the women that Jesus had told them many times He would die and rise from the dead.

MARK
(AD 29–33)

SUMMARY: Unlike Matthew, Mark was not one of Jesus' twelve disciples. He was a young boy during Jesus' ministry. Later, he assisted the apostle Peter as he preached in Rome. Mark wrote to Gentiles, focusing especially on Jesus' actions that would have strongly appealed to Romans. Since Mark covers much of the same ground as Matthew (and Luke), we will look at aspects of Jesus' life and ministry we did not cover in Matthew.

❖ JESUS VERSUS SATAN
MARK 1

Matthew, Mark, and Luke each include accounts of demon possession. Demons—fallen angels—were very active in New Testament times, setting the stage for the great battle between the serpent and the woman's seed, Jesus Christ.

> And immediately there was in their synagogue a man with an unclean spirit. And he cried out, "What have you to do with us, Jesus of Nazareth? Have you come to destroy us? I know who you are—the Holy One of God." But Jesus rebuked him, saying, "Be silent, and come out of him!" And the unclean spirit, convulsing him and crying out with a loud voice, came out of him.
> (MARK 1:23–26)

Over and again, Jesus showed His Lordship over these fallen angels, a demonstration of power sure to impress Romans.

❖ LOVING THE UNLOVABLE
MARK 2

Mark also shows Jesus' love for all humanity—even those His fellow Jews considered unlovable, such as prostitutes and tax collectors. The Jews despised tax collectors as traitors working for the hated Roman government. But Jesus chose a tax collector to be one of His twelve disciples. Levi, or Matthew, went on to write the first Gospel in the New Testament. After Jesus called him, Matthew held a feast in Jesus' honor.

> And the scribes of the Pharisees, when they saw that He was eating with sinners and tax collectors, said to His disciples, "Why does He eat with tax collectors and sinners?" And when Jesus heard it, He said to them, "Those who are well have no need of a physician, but those who are sick. I came not to call the righteous, but sinners." (MARK 2:16–17)

Jesus came to save each child of Adam and Eve. Since all of us are sinners, He came to call each of us—Jew, Roman, and every nationality. No matter who you are or how far you have wandered from God's ways, Jesus loves you and won forgiveness for you too.

❖ JESUS CALMS A STORM   MARK 4

Romans were renowned for their military, which was built on a strict code of authority and obedience. Just as Romans were impressed by Jesus' authority over enemy demons who obeyed Him instantly, they would be impressed by the authority He showed over wind and wave. On one occasion, Jesus was sleeping in a boat on the Sea of Galilee when His disciples awakened Him, fearful their boat would sink.

> And He awoke and rebuked the wind and said to the sea, "Peace! Be still!" And the wind ceased, and there was a great calm. He said to them, "Why are you so afraid? Have you still no faith?" (MARK 4:39–40)

Roman readers would be amazed at Jesus' two simple commands. To the wind, Jesus orders "Peace!" and to the waves, "Be still!" And instantly, the wind ceased, and there was a great calm. The Romans would marvel that "even the wind and the sea obey Him" (Mark 4:41).

❖ JESUS' JEWISH TRIAL   MARK 14

With Jesus' suffering and death, Mark focuses on Jesus being all alone against the powers of evil. Mark's Roman readers would appreciate Jesus' strength to stand alone against innumerable enemies and the injustice of false witnesses. Even His strong silence would impress them and the authority in His answer:

> And the high priest stood up in the midst and asked Jesus, "Have You no answer to make? What is it that these men testify against You?" But He remained silent and made no answer. Again the high priest asked Him, "Are You the Christ, the Son of the Blessed?" And Jesus said, "I am, and you will see the Son of Man seated at the right hand of Power, and coming with the clouds of heaven." (MARK 14:60–62)

❖ ON THE CROSS

Mark alone points out that Jesus' suffering on the cross lasted six hours:

> And it was the third hour when they crucified Him.... And when
> the sixth hour had come, there was darkness over the whole land
> until the ninth hour. And at the ninth hour Jesus cried with a loud
> voice, "Eloi, Eloi, lema sabachthani?" which means, "My God, my
> God, why have You forsaken Me?" ... And Jesus uttered a loud
> cry and breathed His last. (MARK 15:25, 33–34, 37)

Again, Jesus shows great courage and honor.

❖ THE ROMAN CENTURION

In Mark's account of Jesus' crucifixion, Jesus stands alone. Everyone else is lined up
against Him. The only one to speak up in His defense is a Roman military officer:

> And when the centurion, who stood facing Him, saw that in this
> way He breathed His last, he said, "Truly this man was the Son
> of God!" (MARK 15:39)

THIRTY DAYS IN GOD'S WORD

This centurion was the Roman military officer in charge of the crucifixion detail, which included four soldiers for each criminal crucified. Centurions were very noble and highly respected by most of their men and the officers to whom they answered. A centurion stating this claim about Jesus would make a huge impression upon Mark's Roman readers.

❖ JESUS' RESURRECTION   MARK 16

Mark gives us a report of the women who went out to the tomb early Sunday morning to complete Jesus' burial:

> When the Sabbath was past, Mary Magdalene, Mary the mother of James, and Salome bought spices, so that they might go and anoint Him. . . . And entering the tomb, they saw a young man sitting on the right side, dressed in a white robe, and they were alarmed. And he said to them, "Do not be alarmed. You seek Jesus of Nazareth, who was crucified. He has risen; He is not here. See the place where they laid Him. But go, tell His disciples and Peter that He is going before you to Galilee. There you will see Him, just as He told you." (MARK 16:1, 5–7)

It was angels who announced the resurrection, not to the twelve apostles but to the women who had accompanied Jesus to Jerusalem. They, in turn, would tell the men what they had been told. Mark ends with unlikely witnesses—Jewish women and a Roman officer confessing Jesus' divinity and His resurrection.

WHAT DOES MARK HAVE TO DO WITH ME?

Mark writes to people not steeped in Jewish tradition or intimately acquainted with the Old Testament. He shows Jesus as a man of action, a man in control, a man not afraid to stand alone against Satan and all his followers to win our salvation. Having won that salvation through His death and resurrection, Jesus stands alongside you against any opposition, empowered and encouraged to share His love as He leads you toward your heavenly home.

REFLECTION: *What do you think of Jesus when you see His courage, strength, and dedication as Mark describes Him?*

DIG DEEPER CHALLENGE:

Read Mark's account of Jesus' death in Mark 15.

LUKE

(2 BC to AD 33)

SUMMARY: Luke interviewed eyewitnesses and compiled their material to write his account. He wrote for Gentiles and focused on Jesus' humanity.

❖ JESUS' BIRTH
LUKE 2

Luke's account of Jesus' birth in Bethlehem is well known:

> And she gave birth to her firstborn son and wrapped Him in swaddling cloths and laid Him in a manger, because there was no place for them in the inn. (LUKE 2:7)

Jesus was born into this broken world, which, sadly, includes poverty, and so shared our human experience.

❖ JESUS RAISES TWO PEOPLE FROM DEATH
LUKE 7–8

Luke gives us two accounts of Jesus raising people from the dead. The first account is from a funeral procession Jesus encountered in His travels:

> As He drew near to the gate of the town, behold, a man who had died was being carried out, the only son of his mother, and she was a widow, and a considerable crowd from the town was with her. And when the Lord saw her, He had compassion on her and said to her, "Do not weep." Then He came up and touched the bier, and the bearers stood still. And He said, "Young man, I say to you, arise." And the dead man sat up and began to speak, and Jesus gave him to his mother. (LUKE 7:12–15)

Luke alone gives us this account. But his second resurrection account is also found in Matthew and Mark. Again, notice Jesus' human touch:

> But taking her by the hand He called, saying, "Child, arise." And her spirit returned, and she got up at once. And He directed that something should be given her to eat. (LUKE 8:54–55)

❖ PARABLE OF THE PRODIGAL SON   LUKE 15

Jesus' parables revealed God's love in very touching, human stories. Perhaps no parable is quite as moving as the prodigal son:

> And he arose and came to his father. But while he was still a long way off, his father saw him and felt compassion, and ran and embraced him and kissed him. And the son said to him, "Father, I have sinned against heaven and before you. I am no longer worthy to be called your son." But the father said to his servants, "Bring quickly the best robe, and put it on him, and put a ring on his hand, and shoes on his feet. And bring the fattened calf and kill it, and let us eat and celebrate." (LUKE 15:20–23)

❖ JESUS' PRAYER IN GETHSEMANE   LUKE 22

Perhaps nowhere in the Gospels do we see Jesus' humanity more clearly than when our Savior poured out His anguish at His approaching suffering and death:

> And He withdrew from them about a stone's throw, and knelt down and prayed, saying, "Father, if you are willing, remove this cup from Me. Nevertheless, not My will, but yours, be done." . . . And being in agony He prayed more earnestly; and His sweat became like great drops of blood falling down to the ground. (LUKE 22:41–42, 44)

❖ JESUS' WORDS FROM THE CROSS   LUKE 23

Matthew and Mark both shared Jesus' cry from the cross, "My God, My God, why have You forsaken Me?" Luke provides three of Jesus' other sayings.

Jesus' first statement came shortly after He was crucified:

> And when they came to the place that is called The Skull, there they crucified Him, and the criminals, one on His right and one on His left. And Jesus said, "Father, forgive them, for they know not what they do." And they cast lots to divide His garments. (LUKE 23:33–34)

Jesus pleads for His Father to forgive all of us whose sins brought Him to this cross to pay the penalty we deserve for our sinful lives.

At first, both criminals ridiculed Jesus, but one fell silent. Then, he spoke amazing words of faith:

And he said, "Jesus, remember me when You come into Your kingdom." And He said to him, "Truly, I say to you, today you will be with Me in paradise." (LUKE 23:42–43)

These words have brought great comfort to conscience-stricken Christians for generations. Christ's forgiveness is free, requiring only the faith the Holy Spirit produces in us.

Luke records Jesus' final words from the cross:

Then Jesus, calling out with a loud voice, said, "Father, into Your hands I commit My spirit!" And having said this He breathed His last. (LUKE 23:46)

Jesus has completed our salvation and happily commends His spirit to His Father's hands as He yields His last breath.

❖ ROAD TO EMMAUS   LUKE 24

Like Matthew and Mark, Luke records the angel message of Jesus' resurrection to the women who had come to the tomb early Sunday morning. He adds a wonderful account of two of Jesus' followers encountering their risen Savior on the road as they were leaving Jerusalem in sorrow:

And He said to them, "O foolish ones, and slow of heart to believe all that the prophets have spoken! Was it not necessary that the Christ should suffer these things and enter into His glory?" And beginning with Moses and all the Prophets, He interpreted to them in all the Scriptures the things concerning Himself. . . . When He was at table with them, He took the bread and blessed and broke it and gave it to them. And their eyes were opened, and they recognized Him. And He vanished from their sight. They said to each other, "Did not our hearts burn within us while He talked to us on the road, while He opened to us the Scriptures?" (LUKE 24:25–27, 30–32)

Luke shows us Jesus' care and compassion and the way He revealed His purpose and mission to two of His followers who were not among the Twelve.

❖ JESUS' ASCENSION   LUKE 24

Luke alone relates for us Jesus' ascension into heaven forty days after His resurrection:

And He led them out as far as Bethany, and lifting up His hands He blessed them. While He blessed them, He parted from them and was carried up into heaven. (LUKE 24:50–51)

What Does Luke Have to Do with Me?

Luke's Gospel shows us the great love of our Savior and the fact that He personally understands all the struggles and trials we encounter in this life—because He encountered them as well. But Jesus is also the mighty Son of God who has conquered our enemies and now sits at the right hand of God the Father, ruling all things in heaven and on earth for the benefit of His believers, the Church.

REFLECTION: *What comfort and encouragement do you receive through the realization that Jesus experienced the struggles and trials you encounter in life—and, being God's Son, that He has the power to carry you through yours?*

Dig Deeper Challenge:

Read Jesus' parable of the prodigal son in Luke 15:11–32. Notice the father's loving concern for his older son as well as his younger son.

JOHN

(2 BC to AD 33)

Summary: John's Gospel is strikingly different from the other three. John focuses on Jesus' divinity, the longer discourses of our Savior, and His ministry in Jerusalem.

❖ IN THE BEGINNING   JOHN 1

John states Jesus' role in creating the heavens and the earth. Notice how John's words echo those of Moses in Genesis 1:1:

> **In the beginning was the Word, and the Word was with God, and the Word was God. He was in the beginning with God. All things were made through Him, and without Him was not anything made that was made.** (JOHN 1:1–3)

Then in simple, eloquent words, John describes how the Son of God became human and entered the world:

> **And the Word became flesh and dwelt among us, and we have seen His glory, glory as the only Son from the Father, full of grace and truth.** (JOHN 1:14)

In the original Greek, John's words literally mean, "The Word became flesh and tabernacled among us." Like the ark in the tabernacle, the Son of God is dwelling among His people in Jesus.

❖ GOOD SHEPHERD   JOHN 10

In John 10, we have one of the most beloved statements of Jesus:

> **I am the good shepherd. The good shepherd lays down His life for the sheep. . . . No one takes it from Me, but I lay it down of My own accord. I have authority to lay it down, and I have authority to take it up again. This charge I have received from My Father.**
> (JOHN 10:11, 18)

The shepherd's job was to protect his sheep from predators, even if he had to lay down his life and die to do so. Jesus did that through His death and resurrection.

❖ I AM THE RESURRECTION   JOHN 11

John records Jesus raising Lazarus from the dead. Before that great miracle, Jesus gave a precious promise to Lazarus' grieving sister, Martha, and to all believers:

> Jesus said to her, "I am the resurrection and the life. Whoever believes in Me, though he die, yet shall he live, and everyone who lives and believes in Me shall never die. Do you believe this?"
> (JOHN 11:25–26)

❖ THE LAST SUPPER   JOHN 14

John adds special features to Jesus' Last Supper not included in the other Gospels, such as Jesus washing His disciples' feet. Jesus also taught about the Holy Spirit's work:

> These things I have spoken to you while I am still with you. But the Helper, the Holy Spirit, whom the Father will send in My name, He will teach you all things and bring to your remembrance all that I have said to you. (JOHN 14:25–26)

❖ THE PASSION OF THE SON OF GOD   JOHN 18

When the other Gospels describe Jesus' suffering and death, they focus on His humanity. John focuses on His divinity, especially in His arrest and trials. Consider Jesus' trial before the Roman military governor, Pontius Pilate:

> Jesus answered, "My kingdom is not of this world. If My kingdom were of this world, My servants would have been fighting, that I might not be delivered over to the Jews. But My kingdom is not from the world." (JOHN 18:36)

❖ JESUS' WORDS FROM THE CROSS   JOHN 19

John adds three unique sayings of Jesus from the cross—the first is Jesus providing for his mother's ongoing, earthly needs:

> When Jesus saw His mother and the disciple whom He loved standing nearby, He said to His mother, "Woman, behold, your son!" Then He said to the disciple, "Behold, your mother!" And from that hour the disciple took her to his own home. (JOHN 19:26–27)

The other two sayings regarded Jesus' work and must have been spoken shortly before His death, after He had satisfied God's wrath by paying for all of our sins:

> After this, Jesus, knowing that all was now finished, said (to fulfill the Scripture), "I thirst." A jar full of sour wine stood there, so they put a sponge full of the sour wine on a hyssop branch and held it to His mouth. When Jesus had received the sour wine, He said, "It is finished," and He bowed His head and gave up His spirit. (JOHN 19:28–30)

Jesus assures us we will inherit eternal life because He finished all that was necessary for our salvation, clear down to paying the last penny.

❖ JESUS' RESURRECTION   JOHN 20

John gives us Jesus' first resurrection appearance to Mary Magdalene:

> Jesus said to her, "Mary." She turned and said to Him in Aramaic, "Rabboni!" (which means Teacher). . . . Mary Magdalene went and announced to the disciples, "I have seen the Lord"—and that He had said these things to her. (JOHN 20:16, 18)

He also recounts Jesus' appearance to Thomas, who refused to believe Jesus had risen unless he saw Jesus himself:

> Eight days later, His disciples were inside again, and Thomas was with them. Although the doors were locked, Jesus came and stood among them and said, "Peace be with you." Then He said to Thomas, "Put your finger here, and see My hands; and put out your hand, and place it in My side. Do not disbelieve, but believe." Thomas answered Him, "My Lord and my God!" (JOHN 20:26–28)

❖ THE PURPOSE OF JOHN'S GOSPEL   JOHN 20

John closes the first of his two resurrection chapters with this powerful statement:

> But these are written so that you may believe that Jesus is the Christ, the Son of God, and that by believing you may have life in His name. (JOHN 20:31)

These words sum up the purpose of John's Gospel and each book of the Bible.

WHAT DOES JOHN HAVE TO DO WITH ME?

John reminds us that Jesus of Nazareth is the mighty Son of God who carried our sins to the cross and vanquished them. In Christ Jesus, we have eternal life.

REFLECTION: *What difference does it make for you that your Savior, Jesus, is the mighty Son of God?*

DIG DEEPER CHALLENGE:

Read John's beautiful account of Jesus raising Lazarus from the grave in John 11. Think of Judgment Day when He will raise you and all believers to eternal life.

THE HISTORY OF THE CHRISTIAN CHURCH

In the Old Testament, twelve books record the history of Israel. In the New Testament, only one book shows us the spread of Christianity. The Acts of the Apostles tells the story of Jesus' continuing work through His apostles and believers as He built up His Church and spread the Gospel throughout the world.

ACTS
(AD 33–58)

SUMMARY: The Acts of the Apostles was written by Luke. It describes how Jesus Christ extended His Christian Church throughout the Roman Empire and beyond.

❖ THE COMING OF THE HOLY SPIRIT · ACTS 2

At the harvest festival of Pentecost, fifty days after Jesus' resurrection, the Holy Spirit spoke through the apostles to give birth to His New Testament Church:

> When the day of Pentecost arrived, they were all together in one place. And suddenly there came from heaven a sound like a mighty rushing wind, and it filled the entire house where they were sitting. And divided tongues as of fire appeared to them and rested on each one of them. And they were all filled with the Holy Spirit and began to speak in other tongues as the Spirit gave them utterance. (ACTS 2:1–4)

With the Spirit's power and courage, the Twelve proclaimed the name of Jesus fearlessly.

❖ PETER'S COURAGE · ACTS 5

Peter's transition from denier to confessor of Jesus Christ is remarkable. As all twelve apostles are brought before the high priest, Peter speaks for them:

> And when they had brought them, they set them before the council. And the high priest questioned them, saying, "We strictly charged you not to teach in this name, yet here you have filled Jerusalem with your teaching, and you intend to bring this man's blood upon us." But Peter and the apostles answered, "We must obey God rather than men. The God of our fathers raised Jesus, whom you killed by hanging him on a tree." (ACTS 5:27–30)

The next chapters describe how Peter spread the faith among the Jews.

❖ **STEPHEN** ACTS 6–7

The Church was growing rapidly, and the Twelve found themselves pulled away from preaching the Gospel to oversee the distribution of food to the widows. They appointed seven men to oversee the social ministry. One of these was Stephen, a powerful witness for Christ. His bold sharing of the faith soon had him standing before the same Jewish high court that had condemned Jesus to death:

> Now when they heard these things they were enraged, and they ground their teeth at him. But he, full of the Holy Spirit, gazed into heaven and saw the glory of God, and Jesus standing at the right hand of God. And he said, "Behold, I see the heavens opened, and the Son of Man standing at the right hand of God." But they cried out with a loud voice and stopped their ears and rushed together at him. Then they cast him out of the city and stoned him. And the witnesses laid down their garments at the feet of a young man named Saul. (ACTS 7:54–58)

❖ **BRINGING THE GOSPEL TO THE GENTILES** ACTS 9–10

When Stephen died, a great Jewish persecution arose against the Christians. Many believers who had been staying in Jerusalem since Pentecost returned to their homes across the Roman Empire. They shared the faith wherever they went.

In a special vision, God led Peter to share the Good News of Jesus with a Roman centurion named Cornelius. After preaching about Jesus, something special happened:

> While Peter was still saying these things, the Holy Spirit fell on all who heard the word. And the believers from among the circumcised who had come with Peter were amazed, because the gift of the Holy Spirit was poured out even on the Gentiles. (ACTS 10:44–45)

When God gave His Holy Spirit to Gentile believers, the Jewish Christians could not deny that the Gospel was for all people, not just for Jews.

❖ **PERSECUTOR TURNED APOSTLE** ACTS 9

One of the most remarkable persons in the Book of Acts and the history of the Early Church was Saul of Tarsus. We first met him when Stephen was being stoned to death. He was the young man guarding the coats of those throwing the stones and giving his wholehearted approval. He zealously defended Judaism against the followers of Christ. But as he was on the way to Damascus with authority from the priests to arrest Christians and bring them for trial in Jerusalem, Christ appeared to him.

The Holy Spirit created faith in Saul, and immediately he started using his zealous energy to proclaim salvation in Jesus Christ everywhere he went. As he worked chiefly with the Gentiles, he was known as Paul. Through his work, especially his three missionary journeys in Acts, the faith spread throughout the eastern Roman Empire—clear to Rome itself.

❖ PAUL'S MISSIONARY JOURNEYS ················ ACTS 13–20

God had an important task for Paul and several other early Christian missionaries (including Paul's first partner, Barnabas):

> While they were worshiping the Lord and fasting, the Holy Spirit said, "Set apart for Me Barnabas and Saul for the work to which I have called them." Then after fasting and praying they laid their hands on them and sent them off. (ACTS 13:2–3)

They went throughout certain regions of the Roman Empire, sharing the Good News of Jesus Christ with Jews and Gentiles alike.

Through the efforts of Paul, Barnabas, and many others, the Christian Church was established throughout the eastern Roman Empire, and from there spread through the west and beyond to the barbarians who lived beyond Rome's borders.

What Does Acts Have to Do with Me?

The Book of Acts shows us what the Holy Spirit can do through simple believers. By the simple sharing of faith, the Holy Spirit spread the Gospel throughout the Roman Empire. Sharing our faith can seem intimidating, but as we build relationships at home, work, school, and in our hobbies, the Holy Spirit gives us courage and opportunities to share our faith also. Working through those words, He plants and gives growth to their faith.

REFLECTION: *How do you share exciting news with your friends and family? How might you use that same way to share the exciting news of our Savior?*

Dig Deeper Challenge:

Read Luke's description of Stephen's martyrdom in Acts 6–7. Notice how Jesus gives Stephen reassurance when he needs it most.

PAUL'S JOURNEYS

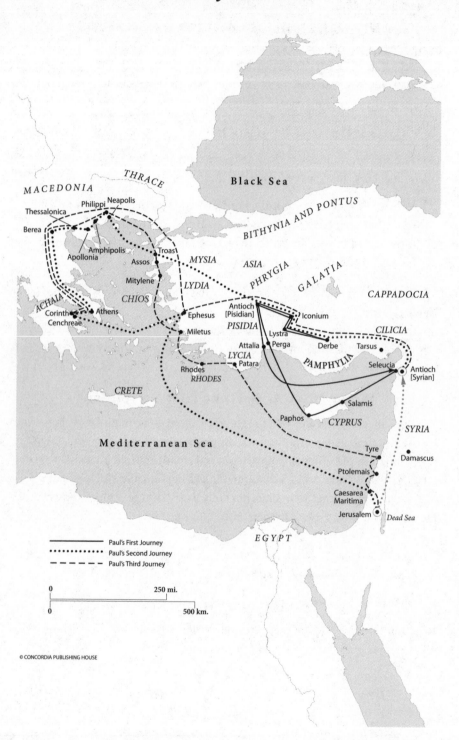

THRACE

MACEDONIA

Black Sea

BITHYNIA AND PONTUS

Philippi Neapolis
Thessalonica
Berea
Amphipolis
Apollonia
Troas

MYSIA

ASIA

PHRYGIA

GALATIA

CAPPADOCIA

Assos

Mitylene

LYDIA

CHIOS

ACHAIA
Corinth Athens
Cenchreae

Ephesus

Miletus

Antioch
[Pisidian]

Iconium

CILICIA

PISIDIA

Lystra

Tarsus

Attalia
Patara

LYCIA

Perga

Derbe

Seleucia

Antioch
[Syrian]

Rhodes

RHODES

PAMPHYLIA

Salamis

CRETE

Paphos

CYPRUS

SYRIA

Mediterranean Sea

Tyre

Damascus

Ptolemais

Caesarea
Maritima

Jerusalem

Dead Sea

EGYPT

——————— Paul's First Journey

················ Paul's Second Journey

– – – – – Paul's Third Journey

0   250 mi.

0   500 km.

The Pauline Epistles

We now turn to thirteen letters, or epistles, Paul wrote to specific congregations and individuals. Paul used these letters to teach people about Jesus' salvation, how to live in Christ's Church, and to warn against false teachings.

ROMANS
(AD 55)

SUMMARY: Paul wrote this letter to the Christians living in Rome before he ever met them face to face. It is a masterpiece, describing how God makes us right to stand in His presence.

❖ RIGHTEOUSNESS FROM GOD   ROMANS 3

In the first chapter, Paul describes the guilt of Gentiles. Though they do not have the Commandments, they sin against the Law written on their hearts. In chapter two, Paul turns to the Jews, showing they have the Commandments, yet they break them. In conclusion, Paul states in chapter three that all people are sinners, and no one is righteous before God, no matter how carefully we try. We all rightly deserve eternal punishment. But where we were powerless to come to God, God came to us through His Son, Jesus.

> But now the righteousness of God has been manifested apart from the law, although the Law and the Prophets bear witness to it—the righteousness of God through faith in Jesus Christ for all who believe. For there is no distinction. (ROMANS 3:21–22)

Paul then explains that this righteousness by faith extended clear back through the Old Testament. He shows that even Abraham, the father of the Israelite nation, was justified by his faith and not by his works.

❖ IN ADAM ALL DIE   ROMANS 5

In chapter five, Paul reminds us that Jews and Gentiles are all united in our forefather, Adam. Because of his fall into sin, we are all contaminated with a sinful nature that gives rise to all our sins of thought, word, and deed, making us unworthy to live in God's presence. But in the one man Jesus Christ, God has united all our sins, laid them on Jesus, and received His suffering and death as an atoning sacrifice. By faith, He gives believers the righteousness that Christ earned for all of us.

For as by the one man's disobedience the many were made sinners, so by the one man's obedience the many will be made righteous. (ROMANS 5:19)

❖ THE STRUGGLE CONTINUES   ROMANS 7

Paul has established that our righteousness is through faith in Jesus Christ. Now he discusses how Christians who have been saved can live God-pleasing lives. In chapter seven, he discusses God's good and holy Law, which reveals the kinds of good works by which we can serve God. But, no matter how hard we try, we cannot live perfectly God-pleasing lives. Paul points out how his own sinful nature drives him to acts that demonstrate he is simultaneously sinner and saint:

For we know that the law is spiritual, but I am of the flesh, sold under sin. For I do not understand my own actions. For I do not do what I want, but I do the very thing I hate. (ROMANS 7:14–15)

But that knowledge of sin drives us back to Jesus Christ and His salvation.

Thanks be to God through Jesus Christ our Lord! So then, I myself serve the law of God with my mind, but with my flesh I serve the law of sin. (ROMANS 7:25)

❖ THE GLORY TO BE REVEALED ROMANS 8

In Romans eight, Paul teaches us how to keep our suffering in perspective by comparing momentary pain and agony with the eternal glory awaiting us:

> **For I consider that the sufferings of this present time are not worth comparing with the glory that is to be revealed to us.** (ROMANS 8:18)

He then goes on to describe the comfort God offers through the hope of eternal life and the specific comfort we receive from the work of each Person of the Holy Trinity: the Holy Spirit, the Father, and Jesus Christ, the Son of God.

❖ PAUL'S CONCERN FOR JEWS ROMANS 9

Paul was an apostle to the Gentiles, but that doesn't mean he didn't care about the Jews. In his missionary journeys, he always began his work in each town in a synagogue, speaking to Jews. In the ninth, tenth, and eleventh chapters of Romans, he expresses his concern for the Jewish people:

> **I have great sorrow and unceasing anguish in my heart. For I could wish that I myself were accursed and cut off from Christ for the sake of my brothers, my kinsmen according to the flesh.**
> (ROMANS 9:2–3)

He reminded the Gentiles that even those Jews who were currently refusing Jesus could still be saved by the grace of the Holy Spirit.

Paul closes his Letter to the Romans with instructions for living Christian lives and seeking unity in Jesus Christ.

WHAT DOES ROMANS HAVE TO DO WITH ME?

Romans is a good reminder of how God saves us by grace through Spirit-given faith in Jesus Christ. It challenges our pride and self-righteousness and shines a glorious light on Jesus Christ, the only Lord and Savior of all.

REFLECTION: *How difficult is it for you to admit there is nothing you can do to turn away God's wrath? How does it help to know Jesus Christ has already turned that wrath aside by taking your place?*

DIG DEEPER CHALLENGE:

Read Paul's prescription for hope and confidence amid suffering in Romans 8:12–39. Notice especially the three Persons of the Holy Trinity and what each does for our comfort and strength of faith.

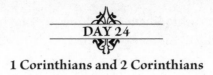

1 CORINTHIANS
(AD 55, before Pentecost)

SUMMARY: Paul addresses divisions and fractures among the people of the church and the accompanying breakdowns of appropriate practices within the church.

❖ TRUE WISDOM   1 CORINTHIANS 1

Paul contends with false teachers using worldly wisdom to mislead and divide the Corinthians. The preaching of Christ will always sound foolish to the world.

> **For the word of the cross is folly to those who are perishing, but to us who are being saved it is the power of God.** (1 CORINTHIANS 1:18)

We should not be overly impressed by people who boast of wisdom and insight but reject Christ crucified.

❖ HE MARRIED HIS FATHER'S WIFE   1 CORINTHIANS 5

In chapter five, Paul addresses the Corinthians' permissive attitude toward sexual immorality:

> **It is actually reported that there is sexual immorality among you, and of a kind that is not tolerated even among pagans, for a man has his father's wife. And you are arrogant! Ought you not rather to mourn? Let him who has done this be removed from among you.** (1 CORINTHIANS 5:1–2)

The congregation's tolerance and inclusion were encouraging the sinner to continue in his faith-destroying sin. Paul calls for repentance and restoration.

❖ HOLY COMMUNION   1 CORINTHIANS 11

In chapter eleven, Paul addresses harmful misunderstandings about Communion:

> **When you come together, it is not the Lord's Supper that you eat. . . . For anyone who eats and drinks without discerning the**

body eats and drinks judgment on himself. That is why many of you are weak and ill, and some have died. (1 CORINTHIANS 11:20, 29–30)

Received in repentant faith, Communion is a life-giving medicine. But it will harm those who are unrepentant or deny the real presence of His body and blood.

❖ THE GREATEST GIFT IS LOVE   1 CORINTHIANS 13

The greatest problem that plagued and divided the church of Corinth was a lack of love. Chapter 13 is one of Paul's most beautiful passages:

Love is patient and kind; love does not envy or boast; it is not arrogant or rude. It does not insist on its own way; it is not irritable or resentful; it does not rejoice at wrongdoing, but rejoices with the truth. Love bears all things, believes all things, hopes all things, endures all things. (1 CORINTHIANS 13:4–7)

If the Corinthians put aside their arrogance and pride and truly practiced the love Christ gave, their problems and divisions would cease.

❖ THE RESURRECTION   1 CORINTHIANS 15

In chapter fifteen, Paul corrects some misunderstandings about the resurrection. First, he refers to the more than five hundred eyewitnesses of the risen Jesus. Then, he confronts the biggest problem—those who deny the resurrection of the dead.

Now if Christ is proclaimed as raised from the dead, how can some of you say that there is no resurrection of the dead? (1 CORINTHIANS 15:12)

He argues that if the dead do not rise, Christ did not rise either. Without His resurrection, our faith is futile, and we are still in our sins.

But in fact Christ has been raised from the dead, the firstfruits of those who have fallen asleep. (1 CORINTHIANS 15:20)

Paul then teaches the difference between our earthly body today and our resurrected body through all eternity.

WHAT DOES 1 CORINTHIANS HAVE TO DO WITH ME?

Paul warns us about divisions that can tear apart our families and congregations. Most are caused by selfish ambition and pride. Jesus' love removes those divisions and centers our hope in Him as we await His return.

REFLECTION: How has pride affected your relationships? How can the love Christ gives us overcome the damage our pride does?

2 CORINTHIANS
(AD 55, before winter)

SUMMARY: Paul addresses issues that are impacting the Corinthian congregation from outside the church.

❖ MINISTERS OF THE NEW COVENANT   2 CORINTHIANS 4

The Corinthians had been plagued by arrogant false teachers. True Christian ministers share the Gospel in humility because they recognize their sin and weakness and glorify Jesus Christ, their Lord and Savior:

> But we have this treasure in jars of clay, to show that the surpassing power belongs to God and not to us. (2 CORINTHIANS 4:7)

❖ THE COLLECTION FOR JERUSALEM   2 CORINTHIANS 9

Jerusalem was suffering a widespread famine, and the saints there were in great need. Paul organized a very large offering from his largely Gentile churches to show their support for and unity with their Jewish Christian brothers and sisters.

> The point is this: whoever sows sparingly will also reap sparingly, and whoever sows bountifully will also reap bountifully. Each one must give as he has decided in his heart, not reluctantly or under compulsion, for God loves a cheerful giver. (2 CORINTHIANS 9:6–7)

❖ FALSE APOSTLES   2 CORINTHIANS 11

Jesus had warned of false teachers arising in the Church. Sadly, the Corinthians were paying attention to them. That tolerance was deadly.

> For if someone comes and proclaims another Jesus than the one we proclaimed, or if you receive a different spirit from the one you received, or if you accept a different gospel from the one you accepted, you put up with it readily enough. (2 CORINTHIANS 11:4)

To prove his call to apostleship was genuinely from Christ, Paul preached Christ's Gospel free of charge.

And what I am doing I will continue to do, in order to undermine the claim of those who would like to claim that in their boasted mission they work on the same terms as we do. For such men are false apostles, deceitful workmen, disguising themselves as apostles of Christ. (2 CORINTHIANS 11:12–13)

Paul goes on to list the sufferings he has undergone for Christ to show that he is carrying Jesus' cross and sharing in His sufferings as a true apostle.

WHAT DOES 2 CORINTHIANS HAVE TO DO WITH ME?

The Book of 2 Corinthians reminds us to honor the teaching of the apostles, the books of the New Testament and to test every minister, preacher, evangelist, and teacher according to the Scriptures.

REFLECTION: *What have you learned about the Bible and Jesus Christ in the past twenty-four days that you didn't know before?*

DIG DEEPER CHALLENGE:

Read Paul's thrilling discussion of our coming resurrection in 1 Corinthians 15.

Galatians, Ephesians, Philippians, and Colossians

GALATIANS
(between AD 51 and 53)

SUMMARY: The Galatians were being led astray by false teachers. The false teachers taught that Gentile Christians must be circumcised.

❖ JUSTIFIED BY FAITH IN JESUS CHRIST GALATIANS 2

Paul asserts that the Law of Moses only accuses and reveals our need for the Savior, Jesus Christ:

> Yet we know that a person is not justified by works of the law but through faith in Jesus Christ, so we also have believed in Christ Jesus, in order to be justified by faith in Christ and not by works of the law, because by works of the law no one will be justified. (GALATIANS 2:16)

❖ CHRIST HAS SET US FREE GALATIANS 5

Paul points out the glorious freedom and peace the Gospel gives:

> For freedom Christ has set us free; stand firm therefore, and do not submit again to a yoke of slavery. (GALATIANS 5:1)

WHAT DOES GALATIANS HAVE TO DO WITH ME?

The Book of Galatians reminds us not to exchange the freedom of the Gospel for the slavery of pride, self-righteousness, and works-righteousness.

REFLECTION: *How would you describe your relationship with God right now? If you are uneasy because of sins, look to Christ. If you are feeling comfortable because of how you are living apart from Christ, look at His cross again.*

EPHESIANS
(Approximately AD 60)

SUMMARY: Ephesus was divided between Jewish and Gentile believers.

> For He Himself is our peace, who has made us both one and has broken down in His flesh the dividing wall of hostility. (EPHESIANS 2:14)

❖ GENTILES ARE FELLOW HEIRS   EPHESIANS 3

The Old Testament hinted at God's love for the Gentiles; Jesus Christ made it clear:

> This mystery is that the Gentiles are fellow heirs, members of the same body, and partakers of the promise in Christ Jesus through the Gospel. (EPHESIANS 3:6)

❖ THE ARMOR OF GOD   EPHESIANS 6

Paul reminds us of the armor God has given us against Satan's attacks.

> Put on the whole armor of God, that you may be able to stand against the schemes of the devil. (EPHESIANS 6:11)

WHAT DOES EPHESIANS HAVE TO DO WITH ME?

Jesus paid the price for the sins that divide us from God and one another. We can turn to one another in forgiveness and love and work together to the glory of Christ.

REFLECTION: *How would you describe the relationships within your church family? How can the salvation Christ has given you transform how you treat others?*

PHILIPPIANS
(Approximately AD 60)

SUMMARY: Philippi's population was mostly made up of retired Roman soldiers.

> I want you to know, brothers, that what has happened to me has really served to advance the gospel, so that it has become known throughout the whole imperial guard and to all the rest that my imprisonment is for Christ. (PHILIPPIANS 1:12–13)

Paul's reference to the imperial guard would resonate with retired Roman soldiers. Every Roman risked his life to serve Rome and the emperor. Paul felt the same in his service to Jesus Christ and His Church.

❖ CITIZENS OF HEAVEN   PHILIPPIANS 3

Romans enjoyed the benefits of citizenship that Roman soldiers had won for them. Paul writes about the benefits of the heavenly citizenship Jesus won for us:

> But our citizenship is in heaven, and from it we await a Savior, the Lord Jesus Christ. (PHILIPPIANS 3:20)

WHAT DOES PHILIPPIANS HAVE TO DO WITH ME?

Because Christ has made us citizens of heaven, we will live with Him in glory.

REFLECTION: *Think of a time you saw the power of people working side by side to accomplish something with God's help.*

COLOSSIANS
(Approximately AD 60)

SUMMARY: Paul counters greedy, false teachers who were trying to turn believers away from Christ. Paul first establishes Jesus' absolute supremacy:

> He is the image of the invisible God, the firstborn of all creation. For by Him all things were created, in heaven and on earth, visible and invisible, whether thrones or dominions or rulers or authorities—all things were created through Him and for Him.
> (COLOSSIANS 1:15–16)

❖ **SPIRITUAL CIRCUMCISION** COLOSSIANS 2

The false teachers were Jews who were teaching that Gentiles must be circumcised and follow the Law of Moses. Paul points to their Baptism into Christ:

> In Him also you were circumcised with a circumcision made without hands, by putting off the body of the flesh, by the circumcision of Christ, having been buried with Him in baptism, in which you were also raised with Him through faith in the powerful working of God, who raised Him from the dead. (COLOSSIANS 2:11–12)

❖ **SET YOUR HEARTS ON HEAVENLY THINGS** COLOSSIANS 3

Paul encourages the Colossians to set their hearts on heavenly things.

> If then you have been raised with Christ, seek the things that are above, where Christ is, seated at the right hand of God. (COLOSSIANS 3:1)

WHAT DOES COLOSSIANS HAVE TO DO WITH ME?

Our Christian life is all about Jesus Christ, who empowers us to focus on God and let good works flow from the new heart and mind He has given us.

REFLECTION: *When you think of your life as a Christian, do you focus more on your own words and deeds or those of Jesus?*

DIG DEEPER CHALLENGE:

Read Paul's description of the armor God provides us in Ephesians 6:10–20.

1 THESSALONIANS
(Approximately AD 51)

SUMMARY: Paul visited Thessalonica on his second missionary journey. After three short weeks, he was driven out of town by jealous Jews. Paul feared three weeks was not nearly enough to establish a congregation amid such severe persecution. So when he felt it was safe, Paul sent Timothy to check on them. Timothy reported the church was prospering by the power of the Holy Spirit.

❖ **THE AMAZING GIFT OF FAITH**   1 THESSALONIANS 1

Paul encourages the Thessalonians to stand firm in the face of their hostile culture. He shares the powerful effect that standing firm in faith has on other Christians, especially under such intense persecution:

> And you became imitators of us and of the Lord, for you received the word in much affliction, with the joy of the Holy Spirit, so that you became an example to all the believers in Macedonia and in Achaia. (1 THESSALONIANS 1:6–7)

Paul did not need to tell people in other areas about the amazing faith of the Thessalonians; everyone had already heard.

❖ **TIMOTHY'S REPORT**   1 THESSALONIANS 3

When Paul was forced to flee Thessalonica, he was worried about the believers there. Would they feel abandoned by him? Paul desired to return to them—but the continuing hostility in that city made it impossible. Paul was worried the church may have collapsed.

> For this reason, when I could bear it no longer, I sent to learn about your faith, for fear that somehow the tempter had tempted you and our labor would be in vain. But now that Timothy has come to us from you, and has brought us the good news of your faith and love and reported that you always remember us kindly and long to see us, as we long to see you. (1 THESSALONIANS 3:5–6)

The Holy Spirit had kept the Thessalonians strong through His powerful Gospel.

❖ WHAT ABOUT OUR DEAD? 1 THESSALONIANS 4

Timothy brought Paul a question the Thessalonians had asked. What will happen to their dead when Christ returned? His answer is one of the most comforting passages at Christian funerals:

> But we do not want you to be uninformed, brothers, about those who are asleep, that you may not grieve as others do who have no hope. (1 THESSALONIANS 4:13)

Paul assured the Thessalonians that Christ will raise the dead first, then transform the bodies of believers who are alive at His coming. Thus we need not fear that our loved ones who died in faith will be forgotten when Christ returns.

❖ THE DAY OF THE LORD 1 THESSALONIANS 5

Paul reminds the Thessalonians that Christ will come unexpectedly, but they needn't worry—the faith the Spirit worked in them will keep them ready for that day:

> For you yourselves are fully aware that the day of the Lord will come like a thief in the night. While people are saying, "There is peace and security," then sudden destruction will come upon them as labor pains come upon a pregnant woman, and they will not escape. But you are not in darkness, brothers, for that day to surprise you like a thief. (1 THESSALONIANS 5:2–4)

WHAT DOES 1 THESSALONIANS HAVE TO DO WITH ME?

The Book of 1 Thessalonians assures us of the power of the Holy Spirit, working through Word and Sacrament to create and sustain the faith He works in us. That underlines the importance of weekly worship for us, and receiving the Sacrament frequently, that the Spirit may comfort us in all our affliction and keep us ready for the glorious day when Christ returns.

REFLECTION: *What things remind you of Christ's return? Why is it important for you to think of that day frequently?*

2 THESSALONIANS

(Approximately AD 52)

SUMMARY: Paul's second Letter to the Thessalonians addresses a question that arose from his first letter. After learning Christ would come like a thief in the night, some Thessalonians worried that Christ had already come.

❖ PERSECUTORS WILL BE PUNISHED   2 THESSALONIANS 1

Suffering persecution for the faith is never easy, especially when that persecution continues and the persecutors seem to hold all the power and prosper in everything they do. It is easy to get discouraged and think God doesn't care or that maybe He is on their side. Paul assures the Thessalonians that God will repay the persecutors out of His wrath. He is patiently giving them time to repent:

> Since indeed God considers it just to repay with affliction those who afflict you, and to grant relief to you who are afflicted as well as to us, when the Lord Jesus is revealed from heaven with His mighty angels in flaming fire, inflicting vengeance on those who do not know God and on those who do not obey the gospel of our Lord Jesus. (2 THESSALONIANS 1:6–8)

❖ THE DAY OF THE LORD   2 THESSALONIANS 2

Paul's main reason for writing 2 Thessalonians was to clarify something that Paul was reported to have said or written about the day Jesus returns:

> Now concerning the coming of our Lord Jesus Christ and our being gathered together to Him, we ask you, brothers, not to be quickly shaken in mind or alarmed, either by a spirit or a spoken word, or a letter seeming to be from us, to the effect that the day of the Lord has come. (2 THESSALONIANS 2:1–2)

If the day of the Lord had already come, then Jesus had not come in the flesh, only in the spirit. Then the dead were not raised, and we still suffer from all the ills of Adam's curse. Paul assures them Christ will come physically, and that day will be unmistakable. He teaches that before Christ returns, the man of lawlessness will come with great deception:

> The coming of the lawless one is by the activity of Satan with all power and false signs and wonders, and with all wicked deception for those who are perishing, because they refused to love the truth and so be saved. (2 THESSALONIANS 2:9–10)

121

WHAT DOES 2 THESSALONIANS HAVE TO DO WITH ME?

The Book of 2 Thessalonians reminds us to wait patiently yet joyfully for Christ's return. We will face opposition and persecution, false prophets and deception, but Jesus Christ is faithful. Through His Word and Sacraments, He will keep us strong in faith and ready for that great day of His return.

REFLECTION: *What kind of opposition and persecution have you faced for your faith?*

DIG DEEPER CHALLENGE:

Read Paul's description of the resurrection at Christ's return in 1 Thessalonians 4:13–18. Think of your loved ones who died in faith and picture Christ raising their bodies from their graves.

1 and 2 Timothy, Titus, and Philemon

1 TIMOTHY
(AD 65)

SUMMARY: In 1 Timothy, Paul instructs young Pastor Timothy how to organize the ministry in the Ephesian Church. His letter is a great guide for pastors today.

❖ PRAY FOR ALL PEOPLE   1 TIMOTHY 2

Paul teaches about congregational prayers:

> First of all, then, I urge that supplications, prayers, intercessions, and thanksgivings be made for all people, for kings and all who are in high positions, that we may lead a peaceful and quiet life, godly and dignified in every way. (1 TIMOTHY 2:1–2)

❖ QUALIFICATIONS FOR PASTORS   1 TIMOTHY 3

Paul lists qualifications for the pastors Timothy is to appoint:

> Therefore an overseer must be above reproach, the husband of one wife, sober-minded, self-controlled, respectable, hospitable, able to teach. (1 TIMOTHY 3:2)

WHAT DOES 1 TIMOTHY HAVE TO DO WITH ME?

First Timothy reminds us what a wonderful gift Christ gives the Church through its pastors. Like all of us, they are sinners who need our prayer, encouragement, and support. But Christ equips and calls them to protect, defend, and teach us His truth.

REFLECTION: *Why is it important to remember your pastor is a forgiven sinner and to pray for him?*

2 TIMOTHY
(AD 68)

SUMMARY: The Book of 2 Timothy is likely Paul's last letter. He urges his dear "son" in the faith to hand over his responsibilities in Ephesus and come to Paul quickly:

> I thank God whom I serve, as did my ancestors, with a clear conscience, as I remember you constantly in my prayers night and day. As I remember your tears, I long to see you, that I may be filled with joy. (2 TIMOTHY 1:3–4)

❖ THE POWER OF THE SCRIPTURES   2 TIMOTHY 3

Paul reminds Timothy of the Holy Spirit working through the Scriptures:

> All Scripture is breathed out by God and profitable for teaching, for reproof, for correction, and for training in righteousness, that the man of God may be complete, equipped for every good work. (2 TIMOTHY 3:16–17)

❖ I HAVE FINISHED THE RACE   2 TIMOTHY 4

Paul believes his death or martyrdom is near:

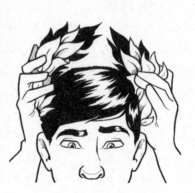

> For I am already being poured out as a drink offering, and the time of my departure has come. I have fought the good fight, I have finished the race, I have kept the faith. Henceforth there is laid up for me the crown of righteousness, which the Lord, the righteous judge, will award to me on that day, and not only to me but also to all who have loved His appearing. (2 TIMOTHY 4:6–8)

WHAT DOES 2 TIMOTHY HAVE TO DO WITH ME?

May God direct our eyes to heaven, and may we have those in the next generation who, like Timothy, fill us with joy and hope for the Church in the future.

REFLECTION: *What person do you know who could use your encouragement?*

TITUS
(Approximately AD 68)

SUMMARY: Titus was a young pastor Paul had left to organize the church on the island of Crete:

> This is why I left you in Crete, so that you might put what remained into order, and appoint elders in every town as I directed you. (TITUS 1:5)

Like Timothy in Ephesus, Titus was to appoint elders—pastors—in each of the town churches on the island.

❖ LIVING THE CHRISTIAN LIFE   TITUS 2

Paul instructs Titus how Christians of various ages should live God-pleasing lives:

> Older men are to be sober-minded, dignified, self-controlled, sound in faith, in love, and in steadfastness. Older women likewise are to be reverent in behavior, not slanderers or slaves to much wine. They are to teach what is good, and so train the young women to love their husbands and children. (TITUS 2:2–4)

❖ WAITING FOR OUR BLESSED HOPE   TITUS 2

Titus should remind the Cretans of the reason for living their lives to the glory of God:

> For the grace of God has appeared, bringing salvation for all people, training us to renounce ungodliness and worldly passions, and to live self-controlled, upright, and godly lives in the present age, waiting for our blessed hope, the appearing of the glory of our great God and Savior Jesus Christ. (TITUS 2:11–13)

WHAT DOES TITUS HAVE TO DO WITH ME?

The Book of Titus reminds us of the importance of good works. Good works cannot earn salvation—Jesus Christ did that by *His* good works: His perfect life, innocent suffering and death, and His glorious resurrection. Instead, our good works glorify God by revealing His grace, mercy, and love to our neighbors.

REFLECTION: *Think of a good work you have done lately. What is the difference between doing a work like that to glorify yourself and doing it to glorify Jesus?*

PHILEMON
(Approximately AD 60)

SUMMARY: Paul wrote this letter to urge Philemon to forgive his runaway slave, Onesimus, and receive him back as a brother in Christ.

❖ IF HE WRONGED YOU   PHILEMON 1

Paul could have commanded Philemon to forgive Onesimus, but he knew forgiveness must be done out of Christian love, inspired by the Gospel. Paul recognizes that Onesimus might have stolen from Philemon when he ran away to Rome.

> **If he has wronged you at all, or owes you anything, charge that to my account. I, Paul, write this with my own hand: I will repay it—to say nothing of your owing me even your own self.** (PHILEMON 1:18–19)

Philemon had refreshed the hearts of his Christian brothers and sisters by his deeds of love and mercy. Now Paul asks for one more deed to refresh Paul's heart—to forgive Onesimus.

WHAT DOES PHILEMON HAVE TO DO WITH ME?

Like Onesimus, we deserve punishment—but God has freed us in Christ Jesus and made us useful. Through our acts of love toward one another, we truly refresh the hearts of our Christian brothers and sisters—especially when we forgive one another from the heart.

REFLECTION: *Think of someone who hurt you deeply. Perhaps you find it difficult to be civil, let alone to forgive. How can remembering Jesus' love for lost sinners like us help us to forgive those who sin against us?*

DIG DEEPER CHALLENGE:

Read Paul's brief letter to Philemon. Think of your relationship with people you have sinned against and those who have sinned against you.

The General Epistles

We now turn to the final nine books of the Bible. These were written by a variety of apostles to various congregations to give us comfort and hope amid suffering and opposition.

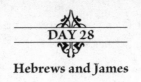

HEBREWS

(Before AD 70)

SUMMARY: We saw that most of Paul's letters received their names from the recipients of his letters. The Book of Hebrews is the same. We do not know who the author was, but everything in the letter fits perfectly with what the apostles teach in the rest of the New Testament.

This letter was written to Jewish Christians who were facing severe persecution for Christ and who were considering returning to the "safety" of Judaism. Perhaps some even wondered if God was using this persecution to tell them they had been wrong to depart from Judaism and follow Christ. So Hebrews works through the highest institutions and people of the Old Testament, proving that Jesus Christ is vastly superior to Moses, the temple, and even the angels in the Old Testament.

❖ JESUS, THE SON OF GOD   HEBREWS 1

Hebrews begins by showing Jesus' superiority over the Old Testament prophets we surveyed several days ago:

> Long ago, at many times and in many ways, God spoke to our father by the prophets, but in these last days He has spoken to us by His Son, whom He appointed the heir of all things, through whom also He created the world. He is the radiance of the glory of God and the exact imprint of His nature, and He upholds the universe by the word of His power. After making purification for sins, He sat down at the right hand of the Majesty on high.
> (HEBREWS 1:1–3)

❖ SUPERIOR TO THE ANGELS   HEBREWS 1

After establishing Jesus' divinity, the author compares Him to the angels who often appeared in the Old Testament:

> Of the angels He says, "He makes His angels winds, and His ministers a flame of fire." But of the Son He says, "Your throne,

O God, is forever and ever, the scepter of uprightness is the scepter of Your Kingdom." (HEBREWS 1:7–8)

The angels brought God's Law to Moses, but Jesus has brought us the Gospel of God's salvation.

❖ GREATER THAN MOSES   HEBREWS 3

Of all the Old Testament prophets, none was greater than Moses. Yet the writer to the Hebrews says,

> For Jesus has been counted worthy of more glory than Moses—as much more glory as the builder of a house has more honor than the house itself. (For every house is built by someone, but the builder of all things is God.) Now Moses was faithful in all God's house as a servant, to testify to the things that were to be spoken later, but Christ is faithful over God's house as a Son. And we are His house, if indeed we hold fast our confidence and our boasting in our hope. (HEBREWS 3:3–6)

The writer reminds the Hebrews of the generation who disobeyed Moses and died in the wilderness. A worse fate awaits those who disobey Jesus Christ.

❖ JESUS, THE GREAT HIGH PRIEST   HEBREWS 7

For Jews, the greatest religious figure was the high priest, a descendant of Moses' brother, Aaron. So the writer compares Jesus' high priesthood to that of Aaron's sons.

> The former priests were many in number, because they were prevented by death from continuing in office, but He holds His priesthood permanently, because He continues forever. Consequently, He is able to save to the uttermost those who draw near to God through Him, since He always lives to make intercession for them. (HEBREWS 7:23–25)

❖ JESUS, THE GREATEST SACRIFICE   HEBREWS 10

The Jewish temple was the site of the many Jewish sacrifices. But Christ crucified is a far greater sacrifice:

> And every priest stands daily at his service, offering repeatedly the same sacrifices, which can never take away sins. But when Christ had offered for all time a single sacrifice for sins, He sat down at the right hand of God. (HEBREWS 10:11–12)

What Does Hebrews Have to Do with Me?

Hebrews masterfully shows us the supremacy of Jesus Christ and the reason we should joyfully reject all other religions and religious systems to cling to Him alone for life, salvation, and eternity.

REFLECTION: *What sorts of things give you a feeling of security in your life? In what way is Jesus superior to each of them?*

JAMES
(Approximately AD 50)

SUMMARY: James was Jesus' earthly brother and the leader of the Church in Jerusalem. In this letter to mature Christians, he discusses the challenges to godly living that come from our sinful nature. Good works flow from genuine faith.

❖ ASKING IN FAITH   JAMES 1

James begins with the challenge of holding on to faith during trials:

> Count it all joy, my brothers, when you meet trials of various kinds, for you know that the testing of your faith produces steadfastness. And let steadfastness have its full effect, that you may be perfect and complete, lacking in nothing. If any of you lacks wisdom, let him ask God, who gives generously to all without reproach, and it will be given him. (JAMES 1:2–5)

❖ BE DOERS OF THE WORD   JAMES 1

James calls on Christians to not only hear but also obey the Word of God:

> Therefore put away all filthiness and rampant wickedness and receive with meekness the implanted word, which is able to save your souls. But be doers of the word, and not hearers only, deceiving yourselves. (JAMES 1:21–22)

❖ FAITH WITHOUT WORKS IS DEAD   JAMES 2

After singling out the sin of partiality in the congregation, James turns to the fruits of faith:

What good is it, my brothers, if someone says he has faith but does not have works? Can that faith save him? If a brother or sister is poorly clothed and lacking in daily food, and one of you says to them, "Go in peace, be warmed and filled," without giving them the things needed for the body, what good is that? So also faith by itself, if it does not have works, is dead. (JAMES 2:14–17)

James is not saying works are necessary for salvation but rather the faith that saves is active. God moves us to show the same love and compassion for others in need that God first showed to us in His Son, Jesus Christ.

❖ WARNINGS AGAINST BEING WORLDLY   JAMES 4

James uncovers the source of the divisions and hostilities in the Christian Church:

What causes quarrels and what causes fights among you? Is it not this, that your passions are at war within you? You desire and do not have, so you murder. You covet and cannot obtain, so you fight and quarrel. You do not have, because you do not ask. You ask and do not receive, because you ask wrongly, to spend it on your passions. (JAMES 4:1–3)

WHAT DOES JAMES HAVE TO DO WITH ME?

The Book of James is a word of warning to us when we grow content and lazy in our faith—when we are drifting away from Christ without realizing it. James reminds us of our need to repent of our sins and put our trust in Jesus and His salvation alone.

REFLECTION: *How is your life reflecting the love of your God and Savior? What areas do you need to bring before Jesus in repentance and prayer?*

DIG DEEPER CHALLENGE:

Read the description of Jesus' life, suffering, death, resurrection, and ascension as our High Priest in Hebrews 4:14–5:10.

1 and 2 Peter, 1, 2, and 3 John

1 PETER
(Before AD 67)

SUMMARY: Peter writes about how to endure severe persecution for God's glory.

❖ OUR LIVING HOPE   1 PETER 2

Peter reminds us that Jesus suffered and was rejected by man for the times when we, too, endure mistreatment and persecution.

> **As you come to Him, a living stone rejected by men but in the sight of God chosen and precious.** (1 PETER 2:4)

❖ SUFFERING FOR JESUS' SAKE   1 PETER 3

Peter teaches us how to respond to oppression and persecution:

> **Do not repay evil for evil or reviling for reviling, but on the contrary, bless, for to this you were called, that you may obtain a blessing.** (1 PETER 3:9)

WHAT DOES 1 PETER HAVE TO DO WITH ME?

Peter reminds us that for Jesus' sake, eternal life awaits us.

REFLECTION: *How can you look past suffering to your glorious future in Christ?*

2 PETER
(Approximately AD 68)

SUMMARY: False teachers denied that Christ will return to judge the world.

❖ THE PROPHETIC WORD   2 PETER 1

Peter first establishes the authority of the apostles and the prophets:

> For no prophecy was ever produced by the will of man, but men spoke from God as they were carried along by the Holy Spirit. (2 PETER 1:21)

❖ FALSE TEACHERS   2 PETER 2

Peter reminds us that we shouldn't be surprised when false teachers arise among us.

> But false prophets also arose among the people, just as there will be false teachers among you, who will secretly bring in destructive heresies, even denying the Master who bought them, bringing upon themselves swift destruction. (2 PETER 2:1)

❖ THE DAY OF THE LORD WILL COME   2 PETER 3

Peter closes out his letter with a powerful message for all Christians:

> The Lord is not slow to fulfill His promise as some count slowness, but is patient toward you, not wishing that any should perish, but that all should reach repentance. (2 PETER 3:9)

What Does 2 Peter Have to Do with Me?

Today is the day to repent and believe—no one knows the time of Christ's coming.

Reflection: How can your daily sufferings and the bad news you hear in the media increase your longing for Christ's return?

1 JOHN
(AD 85–95)

Summary: John reminds his readers of God's love for us in Jesus Christ and calls us to live out our faith in genuine love for one another.

❖ WALK IN GOD'S LIGHT   1 JOHN 1

John teaches about Confession and Absolution—God's forgiveness:

If we say we have no sin, we deceive ourselves, and the truth is not in us. If we confess our sins, He is faithful and just to forgive us our sins and to cleanse us from all unrighteousness. (1 JOHN 1:8–9)

❖ WE ARE GOD'S CHILDREN   1 JOHN 3

One way God helps us overcome sinful desires is by reminding us of Judgment Day:

Beloved, we are God's children now, and what we will be has not yet appeared; but we know that when He appears we shall be like Him, because we shall see Him as He is. (1 JOHN 3:2)

WHAT DOES 1 JOHN HAVE TO DO WITH ME?

Our love demonstrates our faith in Jesus Christ our Savior. When we practice this love for one another, we walk in the light of God's holiness.

REFLECTION: *How many of your words and deeds arise out of genuine love? How many feel more like an obligation? How can thinking of God's love for us transform you?*

2 JOHN

(AD 85–95)

SUMMARY: John urges us to love one another and turn from false teachers.

❖ WALKING IN THE TRUTH   2 JOHN 1

John encourages believers to cling to God's word and love one another:

I rejoiced greatly to find some of your children walking in the truth, just as we were commanded by the Father. (2 JOHN 1:4)

John also warns believers to be aware of deceivers arising within the Church.

WHAT DOES 2 JOHN HAVE TO DO WITH ME?

False teachings encourage us to indulge our sinful desires. But following these teachings means forsaking Jesus Christ, the only way to God the Father.

REFLECTION: *How can the Bible help you more easily distinguish between lies and truth?*

3 JOHN
(AD 85–95)

SUMMARY: John encourages the acceptance of faithful teachers and their welcome by fellow believers.

❖ OPPOSITION TO THE CHRISTIAN BROTHERS   3 JOHN 1

John sent evangelists to strengthen churches (John was not specific about which churches he sent these evangelists to, but perhaps they were the churches of Asia Minor that are mentioned in 1 Peter and in Revelation 1–3). But not everyone received them:

> I have written something to the church, but Diotrephes, who likes to put himself first, does not acknowledge our authority. (3 John 1:9)

John speaks against imitating evil—seeking personal power and influence in the Church—stating instead to welcome faithful teachers and show them hospitality.

WHAT DOES 3 JOHN HAVE TO DO WITH ME?

We are wise to welcome our Christian brothers and sisters and treat them with respect. But we should not associate with those who deny the Bible's authority.

REFLECTION: *How open are you to new Christians you meet?*

DIG DEEPER CHALLENGE:

Read Peter's description of Jesus Christ's return on Judgment Day in 2 Peter 3:1–13.

JUDE

(Approximately AD 68)

SUMMARY: Jude repeats many points Peter made in 2 Peter. He urges us to ignore false teachers and rescue those who have been deceived by them.

❖ **FALSE TEACHERS WILL BE JUDGED**   JUDE 1

Jude asserts that false teachers in the Church will be punished for their deception:

> For certain people have crept in unnoticed who long ago were designated for this condemnation, ungodly people, who pervert the grace of our God into sensuality and deny our only Master and Lord, Jesus Christ. (JUDE 1:4)

Jude compares the fate of these false teachers with Old Testament unbelievers.

❖ **SHOW MERCY TO THOSE WHO DOUBT**   JUDE 1

Jude closes with an encouragement to be patient and merciful—not with false teachers but with those who doubt or struggle with faith:

> And have mercy on those who doubt; save others by snatching them out of the fire; to others show mercy with fear, hating even the garment stained by the flesh. (JUDE 1:22–23)

WHAT DOES JUDE HAVE TO DO WITH ME?

The wrath of God is coming on the false teachers. Jude teaches us how to distinguish between them and weak or wounded Christians who are struggling with their faith. In both cases, Jude reminds us to study and grow in our knowledge of the Scriptures so we can avoid the false teachers and encourage and strengthen wounded Christians.

REFLECTION: *Clearly, it is important for us to read, study, and learn the Bible. Prayer is important too. Do your prayers tend to focus on daily needs or on bigger, spiritual things like God guarding your faith and His Church?*

REVELATION
(AD 95)

SUMMARY: The Book of Revelation explains the hostile persecution attacking the Christian Church and assures us that Jesus will return on the Last Day to banish Satan and give us glorious eternal life in the new heaven and the new earth.

❖ **THE REVELATION**   REVELATION 1

John begins by explaining where the revelation came from and for whom it was intended:

> The revelation of Jesus Christ, which God gave Him to show to His servants the things that must soon take place. He made it known by sending His angel to His servant John. (REVELATION 1:1)

Revelation describes the New Testament era from Christ's birth through Judgment Day. God wants us to know what lies behind the hostility we face so we do not grow frustrated or discouraged or think He has abandoned us.

❖ **JESUS' APPEARANCE**   REVELATION 1

John describes the vision of Jesus Christ he saw while exiled on the island of Patmos:

> When I saw Him, I fell at His feet as though dead. But He laid His right hand on me, saying, "Fear not, I am the first and the last, and the living one. I died, and behold I am alive forevermore, and I have the keys of Death and Hades. Write therefore the things that you have seen, those that are and those that are to take place after this. (REVELATION 1:17–19)

Then, Jesus dictated seven letters, each for a church in Asia Minor.

❖ **THE SCROLL AND THE LAMB**   REVELATION 5

Next, John describes a throne room in heaven where God the Father sits on His throne:

> Then I saw in the right hand of Him who was seated on the throne a scroll written within and on the back, sealed with seven seals. And I saw a mighty angel proclaiming with a loud voice, "Who is worthy to open the scroll and break its seals?" . . . And one of the elders said to me, "Weep no more; behold, the Lion of the tribe of Judah, the Root of David, has conquered, so that He can open the scroll and its seven seals." (REVELATION 5:1–2, 5)

As Jesus opens the seals one by one, we see the events of the end times unfolding. After the sixth seal, John sees the glorious saints in heaven.

> After this I looked, and behold, a great multitude that no one could number, from every nation, from all tribes and peoples and languages, standing before the throne and before the Lamb, clothed in white robes, with palm branches in their hands. (REVELATION 7:9)

❖ SATAN'S RAGE
REVELATION 12

John describes Satan's efforts to destroy Jesus Christ at His birth:

> His tail swept down a third of the stars of heaven and cast them to the earth. And the dragon stood before the woman who was about to give birth, so that when she bore her child he might devour it. She gave birth to a male child, one who is to rule all the nations with a rod of iron, but her child was caught up to God and to His throne. . . . Then the dragon became furious with the woman and went off to make war on the rest of her offspring, on those who keep the commandments of God and hold to the testimony of Jesus. And he stood on the sand of the sea. (REVELATION 12:4–5, 17)

❖ JUDGMENT DAY
REVELATION 20

John described Christ Jesus judging the living and the dead on Judgment Day:

> Then I saw a great white throne and Him who was seated on it. From His presence earth and sky fled away, and no place was found for them. And I saw the dead, great and small, standing before the throne, and books were opened. Then another book was opened, which is the book of life. And the dead were judged by what was written in the books, according to what they had done. (REVELATION 20:11–12)

❖ THE NEW JERUSALEM   REVELATION 21

With the devil, hell, and death removed, along with all unbelievers, the new heaven and new earth are ready for the saints, the Bride of Christ:

> And I saw the holy city, new Jerusalem, coming down out of heaven from God, prepared as a bride adorned for her husband. And I heard a loud voice from the throne saying, "Behold, the dwelling place of God is with man. He will dwell with them, and they will be His people, and God Himself will be with them as their God."
> (REVELATION 21:2–3)

John describes our glorious eternal home in the presence of God our Father and our Lord and Savior, Jesus Christ.

❖ COME, LORD JESUS   REVELATION 22

John ends Revelation with a promise from our Savior and our heartfelt response:

> He who testifies to these things says, "Surely I am coming soon." Amen. Come, Lord Jesus! (REVELATION 22:20)

WHAT DOES REVELATION HAVE TO DO WITH ME?

Revelation describes the fierce battle between God and Satan, believers and unbelievers on this earth between Christ's ascension and His return for judgment. Though at times it seems the enemies of the Church have the upper hand, Revelation makes it clear God is always in control and the outcome of the future is not in doubt—Jesus is victorious. Satan and all who follow him will be judged and punished forever. So we need only to wait for Jesus' coming—which will occur at the time His Father has chosen.

REFLECTION: *Think of the temptations you must resist every day. How do you think it will be when Christ removes all the tempters from creation (the devil, the unbelieving world, and our own sinful nature) and the only desires we will have will be good, loving, and holy.*

DIG DEEPER CHALLENGE:

Read John's description of God's care for His saints in heaven in Revelation 7:9–17.